Secrets of Scandinavian Cooking...

scandilicious

Secrets of Scandinavian Cooking...

scandilicious

SIGNE JOHANSEN

Photography
by Debi Treloar

SALT·YARD
BOOK Cº

FOR MAMA AND PAPA JOHANSEN

Contents

INTRODUCTION 1

Breakfast 4

Brunch 38

Lunch 70

Afternoon Cake 106

Dinner 140

Dessert 178

THE SCANDI STORE CUPBOARD 207

THE SCANDI KITCHEN 209

ACKNOWLEDGEMENTS 211

Index 212

Introduction

Welcome to Scandilicious, *a fresh and – I hope – fun introduction to cooking and eating the Scandinavian way.*

I often find that when people think of Scandinavian food, they tend to think of Danish pastries, herrings and meatballs, and not much else. But, as I hope you'll soon discover, Nordic fare covers so much more. There's a strong emphasis on seasonal food and using good-quality local ingredients. There's a general view that those good ingredients should be allowed to speak for themselves in dishes with clean bold flavours and minimal embellishment. And there's a distinct feeling that the food should be relatively simple and stress-free to prepare, not least because this lends itself well to the Scandinavian love of impromptu get-togethers, usually involving picnics, boozy brunches and/or cake.

As for what we eat, well, think of heaps of new-season asparagus in springtime, fresh crispy salads in summer and rich warming vegetable soups in the winter; luscious ripe berries eaten by the punnetful in season or preserved to last you through the year as home-made jams and compotes. Plenty of local seafood and fish – fresh, smoked, cured and salted – including, yes, the trusty herring but also salmon, mackerel, trout and sweet Atlantic prawns. Hearty meals like meatballs and mash or fish chowder to chase away the chill on damp autumn evenings. Leisurely brunches of hot waffles or pancakes washed down with fresh juice or home-made lemonade. Add to that a love of really good bread and some of the most heavenly cakes and buns you've ever tasted and you should be getting the picture.

These days, Scandinavian food is a marriage of traditional and modern dishes that are bursting with flavour. In this book you'll find classics like salmon gravlax, *vanilla rice pudding and cardamom cream buns as well as old favourites with a twist, like* Scandilicious *macaroni cheese and Eggs Norwegian. There are adaptations of recipes my Norwegian grandmother cooked for me when I was growing up, including lemony choux buns and creamy* rommegrøt *porridge, alongside modern recipes like goat's cheese and rosehip* smørbrød *open sandwiches and Valhalla cherry-chocolate brownies.*

I really hope that you have fun making the food in this book, whether you are wowing your friends, family and work colleagues with your Scandi baking skills or simply making your lunches rather more exciting and inviting than the standard offering from the sandwich shop chiller cabinet. I also hope that as you try the different recipes, you'll enjoy exploring new flavours and discovering fuss-free favourites, and that you'll love them as much as I do – because they're simply Scandilicious!

Sig x

Breakfast

Breakfast

In my experience, a good day invariably starts with a good breakfast.
Scandinavians take the first meal of the day pretty seriously, choosing from
a selection of seasonal fruit and berries, yoghurt, cold meat, fish, cheese,
muesli or porridge, boiled eggs or omelettes and of course freshly baked bread,
buns and pastries. While few of us have the time (or indeed appetite) for
quite such a sumptuous meal first thing in the morning, I do find that a
healthy, filling breakfast – hot, cold, sweet or savoury – puts a smile on my
face and a spring in my step.

A decent breakfast doesn't have to be limited to weekends and holidays.
If you've got a hectic day ahead, you could prepare a bowl of creamy Bircher
muesli the night before and it'll be ready to eat while you make your cup of
tea in the morning. Or why not whizz up a speedy smoothie for a hit of
fruity goodness? And if you do have a little time at the weekend, try making
crunchy granola or morning muesli bars, and you'll have home-made
fast-food breakfasts for the week ahead.

Whether it's a steaming bowl of Nordic porridge to chase away wintry chills,
the simple combination of home-made yoghurt with berries and fruit compote
for a light start to a summer's day, or my childhood favourite of boiled eggs
with anchovy toast soldiers, a Scandilicious breakfast is definitely worth
making time for.

The secret to making yoghurt
Queen's compote
Rhubarb and orange compote
Apple compote
Spiced prune compote
Plum jam
Blackcurrant jam
Fruit of the forest jam
Vanilla-infused honey
Sweet 'n' crispy rye granola
Bircher muesli for spring and summer
Nordic porridge for autumn and winter
Pearl barley porridge
On-the-run morning muesli slice
Black and blue(berry) smoothie
Strawberry, orange and coconut smoothie
Raspberry, vanilla and ginger smoothie
Banana and cinnamon crispbread
Egg and anchovy soldiers

The secret to making yoghurt

Live, or 'bio', yoghurt is considered a great way to improve digestion, and is a nutritious alternative if you're not so keen on drinking milk. But why would you make yoghurt at home when you can buy it in the supermarket? There are several good reasons:

- *you know exactly what's in it. By making your own yoghurt, you can avoid commercial sweeteners, stabilisers, colours and additives. Home-made yoghurt needs only a few ingredients – basically milk and some friendly probiotic bacteria.*
- *it'll save you money. An average 500g pot of bio yoghurt is about twice the price of the equivalent volume of milk. If you eat as much dairy as I do, making your own can add up to quite a significant saving!*
- *the simple pleasure of making something delicious and healthy from scratch.*

Growing up in Norway my favourite yoghurt flavours were fruit of the forest and a lovely vanilla and wild strawberry variety, but the great thing about making your own yoghurt 'base' is that you can experiment with different flavours and toppings – fruit, nuts, seeds, spices, syrups – whatever takes your fancy. The trick is to balance the slight acidity of the yoghurt with something sweet like banana, mango or honey, or zingy like summer berries, rhubarb or passionfruit.

There are many ways of making yoghurt, but here's an easy method for fermenting your own. First choose a live 'starter' for your yoghurt. I recommend avoiding flavoured yoghurts so that you have a neutral base for maximum flexibility – instead go for plain whole milk yoghurt containing live yoghurt cultures.

Next, choose your milk. I use whole milk since it makes a milder, creamier yoghurt than that made from low fat or skimmed milk, but it's obviously a matter of personal preference. I prefer using organic and unhomogenised milk whenever possible.

MAKES AROUND 1 LITRE OF YOGHURT

1 litre milk
up to 50g milk powder (optional)
6 tbsp plain bio whole milk yoghurt

Heat the milk in a saucepan until it steams and starts to bubble – heating the milk alters the whey proteins and creates a dense consistency. Do remember to keep an eye on it, as boiling milk has a tendency to erupt suddenly!

Once the milk has started bubbling, add the powdered milk, if using – this will make the yoghurt thicker. Then remove the pan from the heat and leave it to one side until it is warm, rather than hot, to the touch (the ideal temperature is 46°C but don't fret

if there's no thermometer to hand). Next whisk in the live yoghurt, and place the milk-yoghurt mixture in a warmed glass or porcelain jar with an airtight lid, or in a thermos. Keep the mixture warm on top of a radiator or in an airing cupboard for a few hours or even overnight – the extra time to ferment won't do the yoghurt any harm. Once the yoghurt has set, pop it in the refrigerator, where it will keep for up to a week. That's all there is to it.

You can use your home-made yoghurt for breakfast or a simple pudding, for marinades, dressings and savoury dips, or even in your baking, since yoghurt is an excellent moistening ingredient for cakes and muffins.
WWW

Queen's compote

Such a simple combination, but with so much flavour packed in. If you have a glut of berries, it is worth making large batches of this traditional Scandinavian favourite, or even cooking it for a tad longer with a squeeze of lemon juice to make a deliciously easy jam. Wild blueberries, or bilberries, are excellent in this compote if you can get your hands on them, but if not, cultivated blueberries work just fine. I recommend that you use fructose (fruit sugar) whenever you're sweetening fruit – it is sweeter than commercial sugar so you can use less, has a lower GI and enhances the flavour of the fruit – however, you can of course use caster sugar instead.

MAKES AROUND 500G

200g blueberries
200g raspberries
100ml water, plus more if needed
45g (3 tbsp) fructose (or 70g (4½ tbsp) caster sugar), plus more to taste
lemon juice to taste (optional)

Place the blueberries and raspberries in a medium saucepan and cover with the water. Bring to a gentle simmer and cook for 3-4 minutes until the berries burst and bleed. Compote thickens as it cools, so if the consistency is already thick at this stage, add a few tablespoons of water to thin it. Then add the fructose, stir thoroughly and allow it to dissolve while the compote continues to simmer. Taste the mixture to see if it's sweet enough. If it's overly tart or sweet for your taste, adjust it with a sprinkle more fructose or a generous squirt of lemon juice, as appropriate. If you're not eating it at once, this can keep in the fridge for a couple of days.

Rhubarb and orange compote

My great-grandmother often used rhubarb, known in Norwegian as rabarbra*, in her baking. Early season forced rhubarb is best for this dish as it is pinker and more tender than that grown outdoors in summer. If you're not a fan of oranges, try cooking the rhubarb in water with a little more fructose and some nutmeg, ginger or star anise for different flavours. This compote is great with brunch pancakes or on sour cream waffles.*

MAKES AROUND 500G

300g rhubarb, chopped into 1cm pieces
zest of 1 orange
enough fresh orange juice to cover the rhubarb (juice of 3-4 oranges)
40g fructose (or 60g caster sugar), plus more to taste
lemon juice to taste (optional)

Put the chopped rhubarb in a medium saucepan and add the orange zest and juice. Bring to a gentle simmer and cook for 5-8 minutes until the rhubarb is soft and some of the liquid has evaporated. Add the fructose and allow to dissolve for 1-2 minutes before tasting to see if the compote is sweet enough. Add more fructose if it's still mouth-puckeringly tart, or a dash of lemon juice if too sweet. Once cooled, it keeps well in the fridge for a few days.

Apple compote

There's something rather magical about local-grown apples – their flavour knocks the socks off most imported ones. Scandinavia has dozens, if not scores, of native varieties of apples, my favourite being the Gravenstein *which my Grandpa Johansen grew in his apple orchard. It was always a treat to look forward to in late August and early September with its crunchy texture and pleasingly tart flavour, just sweet enough to eat without cooking.*

I love the clean fresh taste of this apple compote just as it is but, if you fancy it, you can spice it up by adding cinnamon, nutmeg, clove, cardamom and/or star anise after you've adjusted for sweetness. Just go easy with how much spice you use, as it can easily overwhelm the apple flavour. If you are using whole spices (rather than ground), I would suggest that you tie them in muslin or pop them in one of those sealable metal tea infusers, so you can remove them once you've infused the compote – that way you don't risk crunching down on a hefty piece of clove!

MAKES AROUND 850-900G

6-8 *Gravenstein* or 4 Bramley or other cooking apples (c. 1kg),
  peeled and cored
300ml water
75g fructose (or 110g caster sugar), plus more to taste
15g butter
lemon juice to taste (optional)

Chop the apples into bite-sized chunks and place them in a large saucepan. Cover with the water and bring them to a gentle simmer. Cook for 5-8 minutes or until the apples start to break down. If you want a compote with a bit of texture, then turn the heat down to stop the apples from dissolving into mush. Add the fructose and cook for a further minute or so until dissolved, then stir in the butter. Taste to see if the compote is sweet enough and add a little more fructose or a squeeze or two of lemon juice to adjust it to your liking. As with most compotes, this is delicious hot or cold, and can last a few days if refrigerated.

Spiced prune compote

*Prunes are definitely a matter of personal taste – some love them, some loathe them.
A bit like Norwegian brown goat's cheese, really. I think this compote is tasty enough
to convert a few more to the prune-loving cause, but obviously as a prune-lover I'm rather
biased. This is a great compote for those who want to boost their fruit intake during
winter and tastes equally agood in porridge or on toast. If you prefer a deeper flavour to
your porridge, try using a heaped tablespoon of blackstrap molasses, treacle or malt syrup
instead of the maple syrup or brown sugar.*

MAKES AROUND 400G

1 cinnamon stick
3 cardamom pods
2 star anise
3 cloves
250g soft agen prunes
100g dried apricots
juice and zest of 1 orange
water
1-2 tbsp maple syrup or soft brown sugar (optional)
juice of ½ lemon

Wrap the spices in a muslin cloth and tie with string to create a small spice bag,
or alternatively pop them in a sealable tea infuser, so that you can remove them from
the compote once you've finished cooking. Place the spices, fruit, orange juice and
zest in a medium saucepan, fill with enough water to cover the fruit and bring to a
gentle simmer. Cook for 10 minutes or until the fruit has softened. Taste for
sweetness – if it's too acidic add a few tablespoons of maple syrup or soft brown
sugar. Finally add the lemon juice and serve warm or cold. If you're not eating it at
once, allow to cool before storing in a jar in the fridge, where it will keep for
several days.

Plum jam

I spent many a long warm summer on my grandparents' fruit farm in western Norway where we would pick strawberries, raspberries, sour and black morello cherries, blackberries, apples and pears. But my grandfather's pride and joy were the plums – voluptuous indigo plums, yellow Reine Claudes, crimson Victorias – which could be eaten, juicily delicious, straight from the tree or cooked up to make puddings, stewed fruit or jam.

This jam makes a perfect midwinter treat and is a great gift for family and friends, so it's always worth making more than you think you'll need. Plus I find that home-made plum jam lends itself to many tasty ways to jazz up your breakfast routine. I love dolloping it on my morning porridge or on toast, pancakes, waffles, muffins, yoghurt...

MAKES AROUND 10-12 JARS (227G EACH)

2kg de-stoned plums
200ml water
375g fructose (or 560g caster sugar)
juice of 1 lemon

Preheat the oven to 100°C while you wash the jam jars, then pop them in the oven for 10 minutes to dry and sterilise them. Stand them upside down on a clean tea towel until you need them. Meanwhile place a small saucer in the freezer for testing how set the jam is.

Put the plums and the water in a large heavy-based saucepan over a medium heat, stirring fairly regularly while the fruit starts to disintegrate and cook, ensuring that it doesn't catch on the bottom of the pan and burn. When the mixture starts to look like plum soup, bring it to the boil and then stir thoroughly. Repeat this twice, so that you have brought it to the boil three times in total. My father taught me this method and while I am never quite sure whether it's deeply scientific or simply superstitious about the number 3, it does always seem to work.

Take the pan off the heat, add the fructose and stir really well to distribute it. Put the pan back on the heat and bring to the boil again before adding the lemon juice. Remove from the heat and test the jam by placing a dollop on the frozen saucer and swirling it around. The jam should neither be runny nor too jellified. If you're not sure, try drawing your finger across the surface of the jam on the saucer – if it wrinkles then the jam is ready. If not, then boil for another 5 minutes before checking again.

Decant into the sterilised jars, seal and turn upside down until cool. Turning the jam jars upside down while they cool reduces the chance of any rogue bacteria getting in to the air above the jam surface while it is cooling. Store the filled jam jars in a cool, dry place and once opened keep in the fridge.

Blackcurrant jam

Fresh blackcurrants have a wonderful musky, almost feral, note to them that bears little relation to the super-sweet blackcurrant cordials that children seem to love. This jam recipe marries the complex 'grown-up' flavour of the fresh fruit with just enough sweetness to keep everyone happy.

MAKES AROUND 12 JARS (227G EACH)

2kg blackcurrants
2 litres water
350-400g fructose (or 525-600g caster sugar)

Preheat the oven to 100°C while you wash the jam jars, then pop them in the oven for 10 minutes to dry and sterilise them. Stand them upside down on a clean tea towel until you need them. Meanwhile place a small saucer in the freezer for testing how set the jam is.

Wash the blackcurrants and pluck them – the easiest way is to run a fork down the stalk to remove the berries. Put the berries and the water into a large stainless steel jam pan or heavy-based saucepan, bring to a simmer and stir continuously, using a masher once in a while to help the process along. Let the fruit boil for 30-40 minutes until the berries have dissolved and the mixture is a deep purple.

Take the pan off the heat, add the fructose, stir thoroughly and place the saucepan back over a low-medium heat. Allow the fructose to dissolve completely before increasing the heat to medium-high and boiling steadily for 5 minutes. Remove the pot from the heat and test by swirling a teaspoonful of jam on the frozen saucer, checking that it is no longer runny. You can also test it by pushing your finger across the surface of the jam dollop as it cools, to see whether it has formed a skin. If it hasn't, then put it back on to boil for another 5 minutes before you check again.

Pour the jam into the sterilised jars, seal them and then turn them upside down to cool – this should stop bacteria from getting into the air gap at the top. Store the jars in a cool, dry place. Once opened the jam should be kept in the fridge.

Fruit of the forest jam

In Norwegian this combination of fruit and berries is called skogsbær, *fruit of the forest. The sweetness of the cherries, the zing of the red- and blackcurrants and the fresh flavour of the blueberries, raspberries and luscious blackberries combine to give you a rich ruby jewel of a jam that puts most shop-bought spreads to shame.*

MAKES AROUND 10-12 JARS (227G EACH)

450g cherries (weight before stoning)
450g blueberries
450g raspberries
450g blackberries
300g redcurrants
200g blackcurrants
200ml water
400g fructose (or 600g caster sugar)

Preheat the oven to 100°C while you wash the jam jars, then pop them in the oven for 10 minutes to dry and sterilise them. Stand them upside down on a clean tea towel until you need them. Meanwhile place a small saucer in the freezer for testing how set the jam is.

Wash the fruit. Pluck the redcurrants and blackcurrants by running a fork down the stalk to remove the berries. Halve and stone the cherries.

Place all the fruit and the water into a large stainless steel jam pan or heavy-based saucepan, bring to a simmer and stir continuously, using a masher once in a while to help the fruit to break down. Let the mixture boil for 30-40 minutes, until the fruit has disintegrated and the mixture is a deep indigo purple.

Take the pan off the heat, add the fructose, stir thoroughly and place the saucepan back over a low-medium heat. Allow the fructose to dissolve before increasing the heat to medium-high and boiling steadily for 5 minutes. Remove the pot from the heat and test by swirling a teaspoonful of jam on the frozen saucer, checking that it is no longer runny. You can also test it by pushing your finger across the surface of the jam dollop as it cools, to see whether it has formed a skin. If it hasn't, then put it back on to boil for another 5 minutes before you check again.

Pour the jam into the sterilised jars, seal them and then turn them upside down to cool – this aims to keep any bacteria from getting into the jam. Store the jars in a cool, dry place. Once opened the jam should be kept in the fridge.

Vanilla-infused honey

A delicious way to get the seductive taste of vanilla into your breakfast is by infusing acacia honey with the seeds of half a vanilla pod. Place the scraped pod in the honey as well, for good measure. Makes a great gift for friends with a sweet tooth.

Sweet 'n' crispy rye granola

This rye granola makes a delicious topping for yoghurt but can also be used in recipes such as Norwegian knickerbocker glory (page 48, Brunch) and the dessert dish tilslørte bondepiker *(page 192, Dessert). If you have some stale rye bread then so much the better, but otherwise you can always dry fresh rye bread in the oven if you don't want to wait for it to go stale. If you don't have any coconut oil, just substitute the same amount of sunflower oil and add 1 tablespoon of desiccated coconut to the mixture, so that you don't lose the coconutty flavour. If you can't find vanilla salt in the shops, you can make it very simply by combining vanilla pod seeds with sea salt (one pod is enough for about 225g salt), which can then be stored in an airtight jar with the scraped pod for extra flavour.*

MAKES AROUND 300G GRANOLA

200g stale (or dried) dark rye bread
75g brown sugar or demerara sugar
50ml coconut oil
1 tsp cinnamon
pinch of vanilla salt

Preheat the oven to 200°C/180°C fan/gas mark 6. While the oven is warming, blitz the rye bread in a blender until it is the consistency of rough breadcrumbs. Tip the breadcrumbs into a large bowl, add all the other ingredients and mix well. Spread the granola mixture on a baking tray lined with parchment paper and bake for 15 minutes. Allow to cool and crisp up before eating with yoghurt or sprinkling over muesli for that extra crunch. This keeps very well in an airtight jar for a week – if you can resist eating it all in one go, that is.

Bircher muesli
for spring and summer

Bircher muesli is one of those slightly scary sounding health foods that tastes much better than you might imagine. This recipe combines oats, grated apple, milk and a little bio yoghurt for probiotic goodness – but do make sure you use large rolled oats as small porridge oats will simply turn into mush. I find that bircher muesli lasts well for a couple of days in a sealed container in the fridge. If it starts to look a bit solid after a day or so, just stir in a little water, milk or apple juice to freshen it up.

When you're ready to eat it, why not try some different toppings: seasonal fruit (summer berries, bananas, passionfruit, kiwis or sliced oranges), nuts (almonds and walnuts are my favourites for this) and seeds (linseed, sesame, sunflower and pumpkin all work well). Vanilla-infused acacia honey tastes delicious drizzled over this muesli, or you could top it with maple syrup, rosehip syrup, pomegranate molasses or even fruit compotes.
Let your creativity run riot!

MAKES 4-5 SERVINGS

225g large rolled oats
2 grated Empire, Granny Smith or similarly tart, crisp apples
enough milk to cover
2 tbsp plain bio yoghurt

Mix the oats and grated apple together in a large bowl or tupperware container and then add enough milk to cover. I use whole unhomogenised milk as I think it has the best flavour, but obviously it's a matter of personal preference. Stir the yoghurt through so that everything is well combined and cover the container with clingfilm or a lid (as appropriate). Be aware that the oats will swell during the night, so make sure you don't fill it all the way to the top!

In the morning, take your portion out and top with whatever takes your fancy.

Nordic porridge
for autumn and winter

There's a Norwegian dish called rømmegrøt *which gets translated in to English rather unappetizingly as 'sour cream porridge'. It was one of Grandma Johansen's specialities but she never wrote the recipe down, so one afternoon I spent a few happy hours watching her make traditional* rømmegrøt *– basically we're talking indecent quantities of sour cream, some whole milk, a couple of tablespoons of semolina and a liberal pinch of salt. It is cooked slowly over a low heat and tastes absolutely amazing with cinnamon, sugar and a slick of cream fat skimmed off the top while cooking. Rømmegrøt is traditionally eaten as a light evening meal, so if you fancy trying my grandmother's recipe, you'll find it at page 174, Dinner.*

This is my rather quicker and marginally healthier breakfast adaptation using oats, grated apple and vanilla salt. If you can't find vanilla salt in the shops, you can make it very simply by combining vanilla pod seeds with sea salt (one pod is enough for about 225g salt), which can then be stored in an airtight jar with the scraped pod for extra flavour. Vanilla salt is also great with fish and shellfish dishes.

MAKES 2 GENEROUS PORTIONS

200ml whole milk
150ml sour cream
50g rolled oats or porridge oats
50g jumbo oats
pinch of vanilla salt
1 sweet apple, grated

Bring the milk, sour cream and oats to a simmer in a medium saucepan, stirring regularly as the oats cook to release their starch and thicken the porridge. After 5 minutes of gentle cooking, add a pinch of vanilla salt. Pour the porridge into two large bowls and allow to rest for a minute or two. Add half the grated apple to each bowl before serving.

Pearl barley porridge

Barley seldom makes an appearance at the breakfast table and that's a shame. Barley porridge has a delightfully squidgy, chewy texture and sweet nutty taste, that goes wonderfully with light brown sugar, maple syrup or jam. It takes rather longer to cook than traditional porridge and needs a bit of preparation in advance, so it's great if you fancy something a little different for breakfast on a chilly winter weekend. If you're feeling decadent, try topping it with a dollop of cream or some crushed almonds or hazelnuts.

MAKES 2 GENEROUS PORTIONS

75g pearl barley, soaked in water overnight
500ml whole milk
1 cinnamon stick (optional)
1-2 tbsp light brown sugar

Drain the soaked pearl barley to remove excess water. Bring the milk with the cinnamon stick in it (if using) to a gentle simmer in a medium saucepan. Add the barley and cook for 35-40 minutes over a low-medium heat, stirring occasionally to prevent the grains from sticking to the bottom of the pan. Taste to see whether the barley is cooked through: the grains should be chewy but not hard – do remember that it's meant to have more texture than normal oat porridge.

Just before eating, add light brown sugar and a pinch of salt to the porridge, stir through and serve warm.

On-the-run morning muesli slice

Let's face it, some mornings you don't have the time or inclination to prepare a wholesome bowl of porridge – you're running late, there's nothing in the fridge or you're too tired (or hungover) to think about cooking – but that doesn't mean you have to miss out on oaty goodness for breakfast. This tasty blend of buttery vanilla cake and crunchy flapjack is ridiculously easy to make and better for you than many commercial breakfast bars. You can vary the flavours by using different seeds (try linseeds, sunflower, sesame, hemp and pumpkin) and dried berries (I'm a big fan of blueberries, blackcurrants, cranberries and sour cherries). With a little forward planning, you can have an indulgent breakfast treat ready to grab on your way out of the door.

MAKES 8 LARGE SLICES

125g butter
125g light brown sugar
1 large egg
5 tbsp plain bio yoghurt
1 tsp vanilla extract
100g refined spelt (or plain) flour
100g wholemeal spelt (or wheat) flour
1 tsp baking powder
¼ tsp bicarbonate of soda
¼ tsp sea salt
100g muesli
75g mixed dried summer berries
50g mixed seeds
30g dried unsweetened shredded coconut

Preheat the oven to 200°C/180°C fan/gas mark 6. Lightly oil a 15cm x 30cm shallow brownie tin.

In a medium bowl cream the butter and brown sugar with an electric beater until pale and fluffy. Add the egg, yoghurt and vanilla along with one heaped tablespoon of the refined flour to prevent curdling and beat again. Then add the rest of the refined flour, the wholemeal flour, both raising agents and the salt and beat until the mixture looks smooth and there are no floury lumps. Fold the muesli, dried berries, seeds and coconut thoroughly into the mixture and spoon in to the brownie tin.

Bake on the top shelf of the oven for 15-20 minutes until it looks golden brown and feels firm to the touch. Cool in the tin on a wire rack to room temperature before slicing. This will keep in an airtight container or wrapped in aluminum foil for 3-4 days.

Black and blue(berry) smoothie

Anyone who ever thought smoothies were boring should try this indigo bombshell. Native to the Caucasus mountains and readily available across Scandinavia, kefir *milk is a probiotic drink with a pleasing spritz or fizz on account of natural yeasts bubbling away happily in it. My grandmother, who lived to the ripe old age of 89, swore by its extraordinary health-boosting properties. If you can't get your hands on any* kefir, *use any plain fermented probiotic drink or a 50:50 mix of plain yoghurt and milk instead.*

MAKES 2 SERVINGS

large handful blackberries
large handful blueberries
200ml *kefir*
1 large ripe banana
4 tbsp maple syrup
juice of 1 lemon

Blitz all the ingredients together in a blender and taste. If the smoothie is too sweet, add a squirt more lemon juice; if it's too acidic, add some more maple syrup. Once it's just right, pour into two glasses and enjoy!

Strawberry, orange and coconut smoothie

Coconut milk is a great alternative to dairy, and the creamy combination of coconut milk and yoghurt makes the perfect partner for juicy ripe strawberries. Add a zing of citrus and a hint of cinnamon spice and there's some serious alchemy going on in this smoothie.

MAKES 2 SERVINGS

large handful ripe strawberries
juice of 4 oranges
100ml coconut milk
200ml coconut yoghurt
juice of ½ lemon
½ tsp cinnamon

Simply throw all the ingredients in a blender, whizz them up and serve straight away.

Raspberry, vanilla
and ginger smoothie

*A smoothie that packs a real punch, for mornings when your tastebuds need a jolt.
Adjust the amount of fresh ginger to taste, depending on how fiery you like your smoothie.
If you don't have any vanilla yoghurt, use plain yoghurt with a dash of vanilla
extract instead.*

MAKES 2 SERVINGS

75g fresh or frozen raspberries
200ml vanilla yoghurt
2-3 tbsp oats
1 banana
1-2 tsp grated ginger
juice of 2 oranges
1 tsp peanut butter

Just put all the ingredients in a
blender, blitz until smooth and
drink immediately!

VARIATIONS

* Experiment with different fruit combinations – instead of raspberries, why not
use blueberries or blackberries? Ripe mangoes, peaches and nectarines are delicious
in this smoothie and passionfruit is always a winner, but kiwi is most definitely not
as it goes a horrible sludgy colour when mixed with orange juice!

* If you're not a fan of peanut butter, try almond, walnut, cashew, brazil or
macadamia nut butter.

* Instead of ginger, play around with other spices such as cinnamon, cardamom,
nutmeg or even chilli (it may be a bit too fiery for some in the morning, but if you
like Bloody Marys then why not?).

* Ring the changes by using apple, pomegranate, blueberry or cranberry juice
instead of orange. If you like your smoothie quite tart, as I do, try adding the juice
of half a lemon – it works really well with the ginger.

Banana and cinnamon crispbread

I have a childlike love of bananas on bread and this is a riff on something I used to eat as a kid. The nuttiness of sourdough crispbread marries perfectly with sweet bananas, honey and cinnamon. Hazelnuts, if you like them, are just the cherry on top, so to speak! You'll find the recipe for vanilla-infused honey at page 21, Breakfast, but of course you could use normal honey if you prefer. If you can't get hold of sourdough crispbread, try this on thinly sliced sourdough or rye toast instead.

MAKES 2 SERVINGS

4 pieces sourdough crispbread
butter
2 ripe bananas, sliced
cinnamon
roasted hazelnuts (optional)
vanilla-infused honey

Put two crispbreads on each plate, slather with butter and assemble the sliced bananas on top. Sprinkle cinnamon over the bananas, chopped roast hazelnuts if you're looking for extra crunch, and finally drizzle with the vanilla-infused honey. Eat with enthusiasm (and sticky fingers).

Egg and anchovy soldiers

*Every morning in wintertime my father would eat two slices of buttered wholemeal
toast topped with Swedish Abba anchovies (I kid you not) and two soft-boiled eggs.
As a toddler I was fascinated by this. One snowy winter's morning I climbed up on his
lap and demanded a bite of his eggy anchovy breakfast. Much to my parents' surprise,
I didn't spit it straight out, but instead polished off the anchovy toast and demanded more.
From that day on my mother made a portion for me too, and it's still my
favourite breakfast.*

MAKES 1 PORTION

    1 or 2 medium room-temperature eggs
    1 or 2 slices wholemeal sourdough or rye bread
    butter
    Abba anchovies
    sprig dill (optional)

Bring a small saucepan of water to the boil, add the eggs and simmer on a medium
heat for 5 minutes (or 6-7 minutes if they are on the large side). Drain the eggs and
then rinse them in cold water for a few seconds to stop them from further cooking.

Then simply toast your bread, butter it and add as much anchovy as you like,
smearing it in so it blends with the butter. Add the sprig of dill if you care for it.
Slice the toast into long rectangles or on the diagonal across the toast, dunk in the
soft-boiled egg and consider yourself a card-carrying convert to true Viking fare!

Brunch

Brunch

I often wax lyrical about the joys of lazy brunches: meals that stretch in a languid, leisurely fashion from mid-morning until well in to the afternoon; meals where there are lots of different flavours – sweet and savoury – ensuring that there is something for everyone. I love laid-back brunches, spending time with good friends and family, enjoying the ebb and flow of conversation and sharing great food until no one can manage another mouthful of waffle or even the tiniest of pancakes (well, maybe just one more).

In true Scandi style, I tend to lay out a *smörgåsbord* buffet for brunch, with a variety of dishes from which everyone can help themselves. Muffins, pancakes and cinnamon buns are always popular, as are hot treats like Eggs Norwegian, Nordic French toast and buttery baked eggs. Throw in some smoked salmon or prawns and wash it all down with fresh juice, home-made lemonade or a zingy Bloody Mary and you have a *smörgåsbord* brunch fit for a Viking.

But brunch isn't always a clan gathering or a party – sitting down with an ice-cold creamy milkshake and a plate of piping hot waffles all to myself, with nothing more strenuous planned than reading the Sunday papers, is one of my favourite weekend indulgences… and a dish of roasted asparagus covered in golden melting cheese tastes just as good for one or two as it does for ten, but with a lot less washing up!

Scandinavian Bloody Mary

The Green Goddess: minted cucumber, ginger
and apple juice

The Pink Pick-me-up: clementine, grapefruit, beetroot
and raspberry juice

Raspberry and rhubarb lemonade

Banana, coconut and chocolate milkshake

Norwegian knickerbocker glory

Raspberry crunch muffins

Cinnamon spelt pancakes

Vanilla and sour cream waffles

Cinnamon and chestnut bread

Arme riddere cinnamon toast with strawberries and cream

Eggs Norwegian

Roast asparagus with *Västerbotten* cheese

Grilled *brunost* on toast

Jarlsberg and fennel muffins

Baked eggs with anchovy and allspice

Smoked salmon tartare

Prawns on the rocks

Scandinavian Bloody Mary

A brunch classic with a Scandinavian twist courtesy of the aquavit and dill. Aquavit (or akvavit) is the Scandinavian answer to whisky. The name even comes from the same source, aqua v tae, *meaning 'water of life', and there are many who swear by its restorative powers – in 1528 a Danish nobleman even claimed that it '…can alleviate all ills a man's body can have'! Aquavit is usually flavoured with citrus fruits, herbs and spices, most often caraway, cardamom, cumin, dill, coriander or star anise. I tend to use Aalborg Jubilæums Akvavit for this recipe, as its dill and coriander flavours work really well with the other ingredients. Time-saving tip: if you are making Bloody Marys for a party, just increase the quantities and make a pitcherful.*

SERVES 2

    2 shots aquavit
    400ml good quality tomato juice
    1 tsp horseradish sauce
    juice of ½ lemon
    few sprigs dill, roughly chopped (plus more to garnish)
    Tabasco sauce
    Worcestershire sauce
    2 cucumber sticks

Pour the aquavit and the tomato juice in to a jug. Add the horseradish, lemon juice and most of the fresh dill and stir well. Add as much or as little Tabasco and Worcester sauce as takes your fancy, and season to taste with salt and pepper. Mix thoroughly and taste again to check the balance of flavours: it should be spicy, salty and full of umami (the fifth taste, sometimes described as 'savouriness').
Pop a few ice cubes in two tall highball glasses and divide the Bloody Mary between them. Serve with a sprig of dill and a cucumber stick in each glass.

The Green Goddess: minted cucumber, ginger and apple juice

This juice will refresh you if you're under the weather, soothe a fevered (or indeed hungover) brow and even cool you on a hot, lazy summer morning… depending on how much ginger you put in, of course. It's also packed with vitamins and minerals, so you can start your day feeling healthy and virtuous. You ideally need a juicer to make this, but if you don't have one you could substitute shop-bought apple juice for the apples and then blend it with other ingredients, remembering to peel the cucumber and remove the stalks from the mint leaves first (you can leave them as they are if you're juicing). The resulting juice will be rather thicker – more of a smoothie consistency – but just as good for you.

SERVES 4

2 large cucumbers
8 green apples
1 large knob of fresh ginger
(5cm or longer)
1 bag mint (c.15g), washed
juice of 2 lemons

Wash the cucumbers, apples and ginger and push them through a juicer, adding the mint leaves halfway through juicing to ensure that they get pushed through by the other ingredients. Add the lemon juice to the pressed juice and serve immediately.

The Pink Pick-me-up: clementine, grapefruit, beetroot and raspberry juice

This inky pink drink is famous in my household for its incredible restorative powers. The citrus fruit and the raspberries balance the sweet, slightly earthy taste of beetroot juice wonderfully. Do beware the staining effects of beetroot though – you may want to wear rubber gloves when preparing this drink, as otherwise you risk ending up with hands like an extra from a gory horror movie.

SERVES 4

8 clementines
2 large pink or red grapefruit
8 raw beetroot (c. 250g), leaves removed
1 large punnet raspberries
1 large knob of fresh ginger
honey or maple syrup to taste

Juice the citrus fruit and set aside. Push the beetroot, raspberries and ginger through a juicer. Mix the pressed juice with the clementine and grapefruit juice and taste for sweetness. If you think it's too tart, mix in a spoonful of honey or maple syrup. Serve straight away.

Raspberry and rhubarb lemonade

A refreshing, dusky pink sparkling drink to serve alongside your smörgåsbord *brunch. It keeps well in the fridge for 2-3 days but I doubt you'll be able to resist finishing it in one go. If you fancy making a grown-up version, try adding a shot of vodka to the mix, or omit the sparkling water and top up with good prosecco or cava instead.*

MAKES 1 LITRE

4 large stalks rhubarb
200g raspberries (fresh or frozen)
50g fructose (or 75g caster sugar)
juice of 1 lemon
2 stalks rhubarb, to finish
shaved lemon zest (optional)
1 sprig mint, chopped
1 litre sparkling water

Cut the rhubarb into small pieces, place in a medium saucepan with the raspberries and add a small cupful of water. Bring to a gentle simmer and cook for 5 minutes or until the rhubarb starts to disintegrate. Dissolve the fructose in 50ml of water in a small saucepan over a low-medium heat. As soon as the fruit sugar is dissolved, remove from the heat.

Push the cooked rhubarb and raspberry through a very fine sieve or chinois in to a bowl. Stir in the lemon juice and then decant the mixture in to a 1 litre glass bottle or several smaller bottles, using a funnel or jug.

Use a vegetable peeler to shave off the pinkest part of the two uncooked rhubarb stalks and pop these shavings in the bottle. Add a shaving or two of lemon zest too if you like an extra citrus kick. Finally add the fructose syrup and chopped mint, and top up with sparkling water. Chill before serving, or serve with ice cubes if you can't wait that long.

Banana, coconut and chocolate milkshake

Milkshakes are wonderfully retro. My mother used to make banana and chocolate ones for me as a child. They were so good – cold and creamily delicious, especially when slurped through a straw until you reached the bottom of the glass where it made that bathwater-down-the-plughole noise, which somehow added to the whole milkshake experience. This is a slightly more grown-up brunch version. I've suggested using vanilla ice cream, but if you can find coconut ice cream, so much the better. If you're a chocoholic, you may wish to add a few more tablespoons of chocolate sauce. This shake also works well with cinnamon or nutmeg instead of cardamom.

MAKES ENOUGH FOR 2 TALL GLASSES

4 scoops vanilla ice cream
200ml coconut milk
2 ripe bananas, peeled
4 tbsp dark chocolate sauce (or melted dark chocolate)
1 tsp freshly ground cardamom

Chill glasses in the freezer. Put all the ingredients in a blender and blitz for 1-2 minutes until smooth and frothy. Pour the milkshake into the chilled glasses and serve immediately. Feel free to slurp!

Norwegian knickerbocker glory

A brunch-time adaptation of the classic Scandinavian apple and rye trifle,
tilslørte bondepiker, *which translates as 'veiled farm girls'. No, I've no idea why it's
called that either. But whatever you want to call it, this brunch version tastes and looks
great served like an appley knickerbocker glory in a tall, slender glass. You can find the
recipes for the apple compote and granola at pages 13 and 21, Breakfast, and the recipe for
traditional* tilslørte bondepiker *at page 192, Desserts.*

SERVES 2

400g Greek yoghurt
100g apple compote
1 Empire, Granny Smith or similarly tart, crisp apple, cubed
several handfuls sweet 'n' crispy rye granola
40g toasted almonds, roughly chopped or crushed

Layer the ingredients in each glass, starting with the yoghurt and following with
a layer of apple compote, then chopped apple, then rye granola and on top of that,
toasted almonds. Repeat these layers until you reach the top of the glass. Top with
a liberal sprinkling of rye granola and serve with a long spoon so you can dig right
down to the bottom!

VARIATIONS

* Try using Queen's compote or spiced prune compote instead of apple for a
different flavour combination.

* Why not add fresh berries, either in addition to or instead of the chopped apple,
for a summery take on the knickerbocker glory? If you macerate them for a couple
of minutes with a few tablespoons of fructose or caster sugar before layering, you'll
find that the macerated fruit juice makes a colourful contrast to the granola
and yoghurt.

* Using vanilla or coconut yoghurt instead of Greek yoghurt works particularly
well with fresh summer berries, adding creamy sweetness to the mix.

Raspberry crunch muffins

The secret to light, fluffy muffins is not to overmix. An American friend once told me never to stir more than 12 times when combining dry and liquid ingredients and that trick has never failed me yet. These muffins are very versatile and taste great with any tangy fruit, so try them with whatever's in season – from early strawberries and blueberries in spring to blackberries, apples or even plums in autumn. The crispy cereal topping gives that extra crunch factor. You can use sweet 'n' crispy rye granola (page 21, Breakfast) or a commercial brand, but if you're using a commercial one, do remember to remove any freeze-dried fruit pieces that it may contain, as otherwise they incinerate when baked!

MAKES 12 MUFFINS

250g refined spelt (or plain) flour
50g porridge oats
85g light muscovado sugar
85g golden caster sugar
2 tsp cinnamon
1 tsp baking powder
¼ tsp bicarbonate of soda
¼ tsp salt
150ml whole milk
50ml plain whole milk yoghurt
100g melted butter, slightly cooled
2 medium eggs
170g fresh or frozen raspberries
100g crunchy cereal or granola

Preheat the oven to 180°C/160°C fan/gas mark 4 and line one 12-cup or two 6-cup muffin tins with paper muffin cases or parchment paper.

Sieve all the dry ingredients together in a large bowl. Beat the liquid ingredients together in a jug. Make a well in the middle of the dry ingredients, pour the liquid ones in and stir lightly with a wooden spoon until the mixture is just combined. Fold the raspberries in gently, taking care not to overmix.

Using a teaspoon or an ice cream scoop, fill each muffin case three-quarters full and top with crunchy cereal. Dust the tops with a little extra cinnamon if you fancy it.

Bake on the upper-middle shelf of the oven for 20 minutes. Test to see if they are done by inserting a skewer in to the middle of a muffin – if it comes out dry, they're ready to take out of the oven and enjoy.

Cinnamon spelt pancakes

While the Scandinavians didn't invent brunch (apparently that honour goes to either the British or the Americans), we have embraced the concept wholeheartedly. Nothing quite says lazy weekends to me like brunch followed by a walk in the park and an afternoon spent reading the papers. Thick fluffy American-style pancakes are top of my list of brunch favourites, so here is a healthy pancake recipe for winter weekends. Try them with rhubarb and orange compote (page 12, Breakfast) and a dollop of crème fraiche or with fresh berries and Greek yoghurt, or even with the traditional American combination of bacon and maple syrup. I use spelt flour for these pancakes because I think it gives a better texture and flavour; however, if you can't get hold of spelt flour, you can use plain and wholemeal wheat flour instead.

SERVES 4

250g wholemeal spelt flour
150g refined spelt flour
1 tsp bicarbonate of soda
1 tsp salt
2 tbsp golden caster sugar
2 tsp cinnamon
350ml whole milk
50ml plain yoghurt
50g melted butter, slightly cooled
2 medium eggs
butter and vegetable oil for frying

Sift all the dry ingredients in to a large bowl and then stir so that the raising agent, salt, sugar and cinnamon are evenly distributed. Make a well in the middle, add all the liquid ingredients and stir to incorporate into the dry ingredients. Set aside for 30 minutes –this allows the starch cells in the flour to expand and makes a better batter and thicker pancakes.

When you are ready to start cooking, preheat the oven to lowest setting to keep the pancakes warm.

Melt 1 teaspoon of butter and 1 teaspoon of vegetable oil together in a large flat frying or sauté pan (ideally a crêpe pan) over a medium-high heat. Once the fat is hot, place a small ladleful of batter in the centre of the pan and then fry over a medium heat. The batter will sit quite thickly and should bubble as it cooks. When the edges of the pancake start to turn golden, flip it over to cook the other side.

You'll find that the first pancake of a batch never seems to be as good as the rest, and that they improve in consistency as you're cooking. Don't ask me why, they just do. In any event, your first pancake should be a 'dummy' one to taste for seasoning. Place each finished pancake on a wire rack in the warm oven as you go along, until you are ready to serve.

Vanilla and sour cream waffles

Norwegians have a thing about waffles and, along with a handheld cheese slice, a waffle iron is probably the one bit of equipment that you'd find in every Norwegian kitchen. Modern ones look rather like electric sandwich toasters, but with a grid pattern on the plates which presses the batter into square, round or even heart-shaped waffles as it cooks. This recipe is a hybrid of my mother's and the winning recipe of the Norwegian national waffle competition in 2008. Yes, there is a national waffle competition. Proudly waffle-mad, the Norwegians. If you don't have a waffle iron but fancy trying this recipe anyway, you could try cooking the batter in a sandwich toaster or fry it like a pancake on a skillet. Obviously it won't look like a traditional waffle but it should taste just as good.

As for what you put on your waffles, well, the possibilities are endless. Jam and icing sugar, compote and crème fraiche, fresh sliced fruit (with or without whipped cream), summer berries and vanilla yoghurt, honey, maple or golden syrup, chocolate spread, even bacon and scrambled egg if you like sweet-savoury combinations – they all work wonderfully. My all-time favourite is the admittedly somewhat strange-sounding but delicious-tasting combination of a dollop of sour cream with raspberry jam and a sliver or two of Norwegian brunost *(brown cheese). Go on, give it a try!*

MAKES 3-4 SERVINGS

230g plain flour
¼ tsp baking powder
70g caster sugar
pinch of salt
70g melted butter, slightly cooled
70ml water
150g sour cream
100ml whole milk
2 medium eggs
1-2 tsp vanilla extract

Sift the dry ingredients into a large bowl, make a well in the middle and then add all the liquid ingredients. Stir together until you have a sticky batter. You'll know that it's sticky enough if it takes a couple of seconds for the batter to drop from the spoon when you lift it out of the bowl.

Set the batter aside for 30 minutes to allow the starch cells in the flour to swell, which will thicken the mixture to give you fluffy light waffles. Then you just scoop a small ladleful of waffle batter on to the middle of each base section of your preheated waffle iron, close the lid and wait until the indicator light shows that they're cooked (or lift the lid a smidgeon and sneak a peak before that, if you're impatient like me). When they're ready, the waffles should be golden and crispy on the outside, fluffy and light on the inside. Serve piping hot with whatever toppings take your fancy.

Cinnamon and chestnut bread

While some people think of cinnamon as a wintry Christmas spice, Scandinavians use it in sweet and savoury dishes year-round. I've suggested adding chestnuts to the filling of this sweet spiced bread, but you can leave them out if you prefer.

MAKES 8-10 BUNS OR 2 SMALL LOAVES

Dough
250ml whole milk
75g butter
300g refined spelt
  (or plain) flour
125g wholemeal spelt
  (or wheat) flour
70g caster sugar
1 tsp ground cardamom

½ tsp salt
10g dried yeast or
  20g fresh yeast
1 egg, beaten

Filling
100g soft butter
75g caster sugar
2 tsp ground cinnamon

handful roasted
  chestnuts (100g),
  roughly chopped

To finish
1 egg, beaten
demerara or natural
  sugar crystals

Scald the milk by heating it in a small pan with the butter until it is almost boiling and then allow it to cool while you assemble the other ingredients. Scalding the milk makes the finished bread softer.

Sift all the dry ingredients together in to a large bowl, sprinkle the dried yeast in and stir through. If using fresh yeast, cream it with a teaspoon of sugar in a small bowl and once it is liquid (about 30 seconds) add to the dry ingredients.

Make a well in the middle of the dry ingredients, add the beaten egg and then the milk-butter mixture, which should be warm rather than hot to the touch, as otherwise you risk killing the yeast. Stir everything together until the mixture comes off the sides of the bowl and looks – for want of a better word – doughy. Place the dough in a lightly oiled bag or bowl and leave it to rise at room temperature for 30 minutes.

Make the filling by creaming the butter, sugar and cinnamon together, then stirring in the chopped chestnuts, if using.

Use a rolling pin to roll the dough into a rectangle of about 40cm x 30cm. Spread the filling evenly over the dough, starting from the middle and working outwards. If the buttery mix is a little cold, you can use your hands to spread it, as the heat helps to smooth the butter out. Then roll the dough into a wide cylinder, rolling from one of the longer edges of the rectangle, so it looks like an uncooked swiss roll.

Using a sharp non-serrated knife, cut the log into 1.5cm wide slices and place them on a greased baking sheet (if you fancy loaves instead, slice the log in half and pop each half into a lightly oiled bread tin). Cover the dough and leave it to rise again in a warm place for 30-40 minutes until it has doubled in size. You can test it by gently poking it with your little finger – the indentation should stay put.

Preheat the oven to 200°C/180°C fan/gas mark 6. Glaze the risen dough with beaten egg, sprinkle sugar over the top and then bake on the middle shelf of the oven. Buns will need 12-15 minutes; loaves will need 30-45 minutes until they sound hollow when tapped on the base.

Allow the buns or loaves to cool on a wire rack. They will last for several days and freeze well, and the loaves make excellent toast.

Arme riddere cinnamon toast with strawberries and cream

*French toast is known throughout Scandinavia as 'poor knights' (*arme riddere*), which is perhaps a reference to the old-fashioned English name for the dish, 'Poor Knights of Windsor'. Wherever the knights originally came from, this Nordic variation on a traditional recipe is a simple and tasty way of using up any slightly stale bread. I've suggested using clarified butter (unsalted butter which has been melted and the milk solids removed) to fry the toast, as it can cook at a higher temperature without burning than ordinary butter; however, if you prefer, you can use butter melted with vegetable oil instead.*

SERVES 2

Topping
1 punnet strawberries
2-3 tbsp fructose (or 3-4½ tbsp
  caster sugar), plus more to taste
juice of ½ lemon
2 tsp chopped mint
100ml sour cream (or Greek yoghurt
  or light crème fraiche)
dash of peppermint extract
  (optional)

Toast
2 medium eggs
100ml whole milk
2 tbsp light brown sugar
1-2 tsp cinnamon
1 tsp vanilla extract
¼ tsp sea salt
4 slices stale white sourdough
  or country loaf
2 tsp clarified butter (or 1 tsp
  vegetable oil with a knob of butter)

Start by tasting a strawberry to see how ripe it is, as the amount of fructose and lemon juice that you need will vary depending on how sweet the fruit is. Halve or quarter the strawberries, depending on their size, and add lemon juice and fructose to taste. Toss them in the lemony syrup and set to one side.

Next stir the chopped mint in to the sour cream. Sweeten to taste with fructose and intensify the mintiness with the mint extract, if using.

Beat together the eggs, milk, brown sugar, cinnamon, vanilla and salt in a large bowl until combined and then put the bread slices into the mixture to soak thoroughly.

Heat the clarified butter in a skillet or frying pan until it is bubbling. Lift the bread slices out of the egg mixture, allowing any excess liquid to drip back into the mixing bowl before placing them in the pan and frying them over a medium heat for 1-2 minutes on each side or until the bread looks golden brown. If you're making multiple batches, it's worth putting the oven on at 100°C and keeping the cooked toast warm until you've finished frying all the slices.

When you're ready to serve, simply scatter the macerated strawberries over the fried slices and top each one with a dollop of minty cream.

Eggs Norwegian

The brunchiest of brunchtime dishes, traditional Eggs Benedict are given the Scandi treatment here with the addition of smoked salmon. Use the freshest eggs you can find – the fresher they are, the more viscous the albumin in the egg white, and the better the eggs hold their shape in the water. Many recipes call for the addition of vinegar or the creation of a vortex in the middle of the water when poaching eggs, but frankly the most effective method is Delia Smith's which involves removing the pan from the heat for most of the cooking time. If you follow her advice, keep the water shallow, ensure that the eggs are as spankingly fresh as you can and keep a stop watch or egg timer to hand, your eggs should poach perfectly and all will seem right with the world. You can add chopped herbs like dill, parsley, chive or tarragon to the sauce if you wish, but I find that simple, unadorned hollandaise is best.

Hollandaise
3 tbsp white wine
  vinegar
4 white peppercorns
1 bay leaf
1 blade mace
2 medium egg yolks
1 tbsp lemon juice
120g butter, plus more
  for buttering muffins

The rest
4 fresh large eggs
2 English muffins
4 slices (c. 100g)
  smoked salmon
chervil to garnish
  (optional)

Put the vinegar, peppercorns, bay leaf and mace in a small saucepan with 6 tablespoons of water and bring to a simmer. Keep an eye on this as it reduces very quickly. Once the liquid has reduced to about one tablespoonful, strain it and keep it warm in a small pre-heated cup.

Blitz the egg yolks with a pinch of salt in the blender for 1 minute, then add the warm reduction and the lemon juice and blitz again to blend.

Melt the butter in a small pan over a low heat until it starts to foam, but don't let it burn. Then start pouring the hot butter in a very slow trickle in to the lemony-yolk mixture in the blender, blitzing all the while. The slower you incorporate the yolks, the less likely the mixture is to split. If you think that the hollandaise is about to separate, add a teaspoon of cold water to bring it back from the brink. Once all the yolk mix has been incorporated, season the sauce to taste and then keep it warm in a covered heatproof bowl over very gently simmering water or in a thermos until needed.

Bring a couple of centimetres of water to boil in a medium saucepan and then turn the heat right down so that you can only just see a hint of bubbles. Crack each egg into a small bowl or espresso cup, lower to the just-boiling water and then gently drop the egg in. Set your timer for one minute, and once that minute is up, remove the pan from the heat. Re-set your timer to 10 minutes and leave the eggs to cook in the hot water – when the timer goes, you should have perfectly poached eggs.

While the eggs are cooking off the heat, split and toast the English muffins, then butter both halves and place a sliver of smoked salmon on top of each one.

Once eggs are cooked, remove them from the water with a slotted spoon and drain by holding the spoon on some kitchen towel for a few seconds. Place each egg on to a salmon-topped muffin half and cover with silky hollandaise. Garnish with chervil if using.

Roast asparagus
with *Västerbotten* cheese

Swedish Västerbotten *is a Parmesan-like, hard, cow's milk cheese with a nutty taste and granular texture. The story goes that a dairy maid living near the north-eastern coast of Sweden in the 1870s abandoned her cheese-making to meet an admirer, and while she was gone the fire under the milk curds went out. Her attempts to rescue her cold curds resulted in the alternating stirring and heating method still used to make this cheese.* Västerbotten *melts well and its strong salty flavour perfectly complements crunchy roast asparagus. I love to make this dish during late spring when asparagus is at its very best.*

SERVES 3-4

24 asparagus, any woody ends snapped off
30g butter, melted
juice of ½ lemon (optional)
75g *Västerbotten* cheese, finely grated

Preheat the oven to 220°C/ 200°C fan/gas mark 7. Line a large roasting tin with aluminium foil and lightly grease with oil (or a little extra melted butter) to prevent the asparagus from sticking.

Place the asparagus in the roasting tin, ensuring that it is not too bunched together otherwise it will steam rather than roast. Roast it in two batches if there is insufficient room to spread it all out in the roasting tin in one go.

Drizzle the melted butter over the asparagus, season with salt and pepper and roast in the oven for 8-10 minutes. Then add the lemon juice, if using, and sprinkle the grated *Västerbotten* over the top. Pop back in the oven and roast for a further 5 minutes or so until the cheese melts. Remove from the oven and eat while warm and crunchy.

Grilled *brunost* on toast

No doubt I shall be severely reprimanded by purist Norwegian cheese-lovers for suggesting that you grill Norway's favourite brunost *(brown cheese) but I think it's worth it, as this is a real humdinger – a sweet and savoury take on traditional cheese on toast.* Brunost – *sometimes called* gjetost *(an old-fashioned term for goat's cheese) in the US – has a soft dense texture and gets its brown colouring and sweet taste from the slow boiling of milk, cream and whey which caramelises the natural milk sugars. I've added a smidgeon of raspberry jam and a dusting of ground allspice to complement the distinctive savoury caramel cheese flavour. If* brunost *is not to your taste, try using a sweet nutty cheese like* Jarlsberg *instead.*

SERVES 2

4 slices sourdough bread
butter
1 tbsp raspberry jam
8 slices *brunost* (c. 50g)
pinch of ground allspice

Toast the bread slices lightly to make them crisp, then spread with butter and jam. Lay the cheese slices on top and sprinkle with the allspice. Then just pop them under a medium grill for 1 minute or until the cheese is bubbling. Serve just as it is and eat while deliciously hot and gooey.

Jarlsberg and fennel muffins

These muffins are a savoury version of sweet classics like blueberry muffins, or lemon and poppy seed, and are so quick to make that you can knock up a batch in no time. This is one for cheeselovers everywhere. I prefer to make these with spelt flour because I think it gives a better taste and texture, but if you don't have any, use plain and wholemeal wheat flour instead. Similarly if you don't have a muffin tin fret not, as this recipe can easily be baked for 40 minutes or so in a loaf tin as a quick cheesy bread, which keeps for a few days, toasts well and tastes marvellous grilled with a little extra Jarlsberg on top!

MAKES 6 LARGE OR 12 SMALL MUFFINS

150g wholewheat spelt flour
150g refined spelt flour
1 tbsp fennel seeds
½ tsp mustard powder
½ tsp cayenne pepper
1 tsp baking powder
½ tsp bicarbonate of soda
1 generous tbsp Marmite or other
  yeast extract spread (c. 20g)
150g whole milk
1 medium egg
40g melted butter
100g *Jarlsberg*, coarsely grated

Preheat the oven to 190°C/170°C fan/gas mark 5. Line the muffin tray with baking parchment or paper muffin cups, or simply lightly grease so the muffins don't stick.

Sift all the dry ingredients in to a large bowl and stir to distribute the raising agents and seasoning evenly through the mix.

Dissolve the Marmite in a tablespoon or two of boiling water, and add to the milk. Make a well in the middle of the dry ingredients and add all the liquid ingredients. Stir a couple of times before gently folding in the cheese until the mixture is just combined. Use an ice cream scoop or teaspoon to spoon the batter into the muffin cups, filling them three-quarters full.

Bake on the upper-middle shelf of the oven for 25-30 minutes for large muffins, or 15-25 minutes for smaller ones, depending on your oven. Scatter another fine grating of *Jarlsberg* over the muffins as they cool on a wire rack. Enjoy hot or cold, either on their own or with soups or salads as a nice alternative to ordinary bread.

Baked eggs with anchovy and allspice

Known as oeufs en cocotte *(eggs in ramekins) in French, this is a fantastically easy dish to make. I find that the hint of allspice picks up the flavour of the anchovies; however, feel free to use other spices or herbs – caraway seeds, fennel seeds and dill all go well. Do make sure you use Swedish anchovies if at all possible (technically known as sprats) – they're milder and sweeter than their darker salty Mediterranean counterparts. Sprats are often preserved in sweetened brine, rather than oil, with a little cinnamon or ginger, and have a soft texture and delicately salt-sweet flavour which marries beautifully with the creamy buttery eggs.*

SERVES 4

50g softened butter
4 Abba anchovy fillets, chopped
¼ tsp freshly ground allspice

pinch of white pepper
4 large egg
4 tbsp crème fraiche

Preheat the oven to 180°C/160°C fan/gas mark 4 and boil the kettle, as you'll need hot water to surround the ramekins while the eggs bake.

Mix the butter, anchovies, allspice and white pepper in a small bowl. Use this flavoured butter to grease four 7.5cm diameter ramekin dishes. Cover any unused anchovy butter and keep in the fridge for spreading on toast or seasoning white fish.

Crack one egg in to each ramekin, season with a sprinkle of salt and white pepper and add a good spoonful of crème fraiche to cover the egg. You can dot a little more anchovy and allspice butter on top of the crème fraiche if you fancy it, or leave it plain.

Place the ramekins in a 30cm x 20cm baking or roasting tin and carefully pour the boiled water around them so that the water comes halfway up their sides. Bake in the oven for 12-15 minutes for perfectly soft baked eggs. Serve just as they are or with buttered sourdough toast soldiers for dunking.

Smoked salmon tartare

There are some weekends when nothing but smoked salmon tartare will do. Perfect if you're celebrating with friends – or maybe feeling the after-effects of celebrating the night before. Partnered with a glass or two of fresh beetroot juice (or maybe a Scandinavian Bloody Mary, page 42, Brunch), I find that this dish can soothe and revive even the most delicate of constitutions.

SERVES 4

400g smoked salmon, roughly chopped
2 banana shallots, finely chopped
2 sprigs dill, chopped (plus 1 extra sprig to garnish)
zest of 1 lemon
1 tbsp capers, chopped
1 tsp horseradish cream
pinch of black pepper
1-2 tbsp vegetable oil
300ml tub sour cream
2 lemons, cut into wedges
8-12 sourdough crispbread

Mix the salmon, shallots, dill, lemon zest, capers, horseadish cream, black pepper and oil together in a medium bowl.

Serve in four bowls and garnish each portion with a dollop or two of sour cream, a few small sprigs of dill and a couple of lemon wedges. Eat immediately, breaking up the crispbread in to tortilla chip-sized pieces to scoop up mouthfuls of the salmon and sour cream, and squeezing lemon juice on to each scoopful as you go.

Prawns on the rocks

At the fish market in Bergen near where my father grew up, you can get the most delicious sweet prawn sandwiches, piled high with the best North Sea prawns. There are no actual rocks in this healthy brunch option – it gets its name from the fact that it's served in a glass like an alcoholic drink. As there's no ice in it, I suppose it should strictly be called 'prawns straight up'; however, that just doesn't have the same maritime ring to it. If you're not a mayo fan, try substituting a 50:50 mix of crème fraiche and salad cream, or even mashed avocado which goes wonderfully with prawns and is full of essential fatty acids.

FOR 2 TO SHARE

butter
4 sourdough crispbread
2 tbsp mayonnaise
200g sweet prawns
few sprigs dill, roughly chopped
small handful edible flowers, e.g. chive blossom, borage,
  chamomile or cowslip (optional)
1 lemon, cut into quarters

Thinly butter the crispbread and divide between two plates. Spoon a couple of tablespoons of mayonnaise in to the bottom of a martini glass, jam jar or small glass bowl and pile the prawns, dill and edible flowers (if using) on top. Serve with the lemon quarters within easy reach. Crack your crispbread in to bite-sized pieces and take it in turns to dunk deep in the prawn mixture, squeezing lemon juice on to each scoopful as you go. Accompany with a glass of chilled fruity wine, such as Riesling or Grüner Veltliner, or refreshing raspberry and rhubarb lemonade (page 46, Brunch).

	89		
	41		
	123		
	77		

Lunch

Lunch

Poor old lunch seems to end up getting neglected almost as much as breakfast these days (especially during the working week), although less so in Scandinavia than in many places. In the majority of Nordic countries you will still find plenty of people who make their own *smørbrød* open sandwiches or fresh salad every day. There is no doubt about it in my mind: home-made lunch is so much nicer, and cheaper, than something from a chiller cabinet in the local sandwich shop.

Why not make lunch an opportunity to have something really tasty to eat that will set you up for the rest of the day? It doesn't have to take long to make… or eat! How about a smoked trout salad to give you a brain-boost, or a Scandilicious egg and potato salad, topped with whatever cold meats, fish or cheese you happen to have in the fridge? Alternatively, try giving cottage cheese a bit of a makeover with beetroot, egg and crispy lettuce leaves – it's one of my all-time favourite combinations.

There are plenty of healthy and delicious open sandwiches that you can make, or if you're feeling particularly peckish, a Scooby-doo-style meatball baguette can stave off hunger pangs for hours. And on soggy grey autumn and winter days there's nothing as cheering as steaming hot soup, creamy and packed full of veggie goodness. After a lunch like that, I think you'll find that you feel ready to face the afternoon with a smile.

Oatmeal bread
Spelt and fennel seed bread
The secret to making *smørbrød*
Goat's cheese with radish and rosehip
Gravlaks and beetroot
Mackerel, fennel and horseradish
Wild mushroom and tarragon
Toast Skagen
Chopped egg and kaviar
Classic herring and potato
Chicken liver pâté with pickled beetroot
Crushed pea, bacon and tarragon
Nordic club sandwich
Meatball baguette
Roasted swede soup
Mama Johansen's vegetable soup
Cream of tomato and cardamom soup
Tangy egg and potato salad
Crunchy salad with lemon and mustard
Egg, beetroot and cottage cheese salad
Hot smoked trout salad

Scandilicious Bread

Good bread is practically a birthright in Scandinavia and the Nordic countries abound with artisan bakeries, where it's not unusual to find 8 or 10 different types of yeasted and sourdough bread freshly baked on any given day. But nothing quite beats home-made bread. Making bread is my favourite kitchen activity and I secretly relish making a bit of a mess while doing so – getting stray blobs of dough stuck behind my ear when tucking my hair back while kneading, and managing to dust every surface of my kitchen with flour. Plus, quite aside from the fun of making it, you can control exactly what's goes in, so there'll be no hidden additives and preservatives lurking beneath the crust.

Whether you make bread with yeast or sourdough is a matter of taste. Sourdough has become rather fashionable in recent years, but breads made with a modicum of regular fresh or dried yeast can be just as delicious and healthy. Yeasted breads also tend to be a bit more forgiving to make, particularly if you aren't a regular baker. I've included two of my favourite recipes here so why not treat yourself to a morning's baking sometime and give them a try? And do feel free to experiment with using different nuts, seeds, grains, herbs and flours. You'll soon be hooked!

If you'd rather make buns than a single loaf, try using a lightly oiled muffin tin instead of a loaf tin. After you've proved the dough for the first time, knock it back and knead as usual, then divide it up and put an equal-sized blob in each muffin tin cup, before leaving to prove for a second time under oiled clingfilm or a teatowel in a warm place for about 15-20 minutes. Bake at the same temperatures as the loaf recipe but for a shorter time, reducing from 220°C/200°C fan/gas mark 7 to 190°C/170°C fan/gas mark 5 after 5 minutes (rather than 15) so that the buns don't burn. Bake for a further 10-15 minutes depending on how big the muffins are and voilà – freshly baked buns!

Oatmeal bread

One of my all-time favourite loaves, oatmeal bread has a really satisfying chewiness and is so moist you can (almost) eat it without the mandatory pat of butter when it comes hot out of the oven. Serve this with cheese or use as a base for open sandwiches like chicken liver pâté with pickled beetroot (page 90, Lunch).

30g butter	225g refined spelt (or plain) flour
1 level tbsp treacle	2 tsp salt
150g jumbo oats or porridge oats, plus	15g fresh yeast
more to finish (optional)	or 1 sachet dried yeast (7g)
225g wholemeal spelt (or wheat) flour	1 medium egg, beaten

Lightly grease a 900g (2lb) loaf tin. Heat 250ml of water in a small pan until simmering, then add the butter and treacle and stir until melted. Stir in the jumbo or porridge oats, remove from the heat and set aside.

Sift both flours, the salt and the dried yeast in a large mixing bowl and mix thoroughly so the salt and yeast are evenly distributed. If you're using fresh yeast, crumble it in after sieving the flours and salt or (if you want to check its freshness first) cream it with a teaspoonful of sugar in a small bowl or mug, and when it starts to bubble and fizz, scoop it in to the flour mix. Have 125ml of lukewarm water to hand. Make a hollow in the flour, add the oat mixture and half the water and stir together with a wooden spoon. When the mixture begins to come together, scrape the dough off the spoon and continue to mix with your hands, adding as much of the remaining lukewarm water as you need to form a slightly sticky (but definitely not wet) dough.

Turn the dough out on a floured board or surface and knead for 5 minutes (ideally using a plastic or metal dough scraper) until it springs back when you press it lightly with your thumb. Transfer the dough to the mixing bowl again, cover with lightly oiled clingfilm and leave to rise somewhere warm for 45 minutes to an hour until it has doubled in size.

Knock the risen dough back by giving it a couple of punches. Knead gently on a floured surface for 1-2 minutes then shape the loaf and put it in the tin smooth side upwards. Cover it with oiled clingfilm again and leave for a further 30-40 minutes until the loaf has doubled in size. It's worth checking the dough regularly if you're using spelt flour, as I find it has a tendency to prove quickly.

Preheat the oven to 220°C/200°C fan/gas mark 7. Brush the top of the loaf with beaten egg then sprinkle with a handful of oats (if using). Place the loaf on the upper middle shelf of the oven and bake for 15 minutes at 220°C/200°C fan/gas mark 7 before turning the heat down to 190°C/170°C fan/gas mark 5 and baking for a further 25-30 minutes. Tap the base of the loaf to hear whether it's hollow, which indicates that it's cooked through – it should also feel lighter than when it first went in the oven.

Leave in the tin for 10 minutes then turn out to cool on a wire rack. Eat with slabs of butter or cheese or just as it is, warm and delicious.

Spelt and fennel seed bread

I love the aniseed flavour of fennel seeds but if you're not so keen then top this with sesame or poppy seeds, or maybe some whole spelt flakes. Fennel goes wonderfully with fish and meat, so try this bread with smoked salmon, hot smoked trout, bacon, ham or cold roast chicken. If you can't find buttermilk, just use 290ml milk with a squirt of lemon in it – it curdles the milk but don't worry, it's meant to.

290ml buttermilk

50g melted butter

1 tbsp treacle or clear honey

200g wholemeal spelt
 (or wheat) flour

200g refined spelt (or plain) flour

1½ tsp salt

15g fresh yeast
 or 1 sachet dried yeast (7g)

1 medium egg, beaten

handful fennel seeds

Lightly oil a 900g (2lb) loaf tin. Heat the buttermilk, butter and treacle in a small saucepan to just below boiling point, remove from the heat and allow to cool to blood temperature (it needs to be below 50°C before adding to the yeast, as otherwise you risk killing it).

Sift both flours, salt and dried yeast in a large mixing bowl and mix thoroughly so the salt and yeast are evenly distributed. If you're using fresh yeast, crumble it in after sieving the flours and salt or (if you want to check its freshness first) cream it with a teaspoonful of sugar in a small bowl or mug, and when it starts to bubble and fizz, scoop it in to the flour mix. Make a hollow in the flour and add half the lukewarm milk mixture, stir with a wooden spoon and then add the rest of the milk. When the mixture begins to come together, scrape the dough off the spoon and continue to mix with your hands, adding a little warm water if you need any extra liquid to form a slightly sticky (but definitely not wet) dough.

Turn the dough out on a floured board or surface and knead for 5 minutes (ideally using a plastic or metal dough scraper) until it springs back when you press it lightly with your thumb. Transfer the dough to the mixing bowl again, cover with lightly oiled clingfilm and leave to rise somewhere warm for 45 minutes to an hour until it has doubled in size.

Knock the risen dough back by giving it a couple of punches. Knead gently on a floured surface for 1-2 minutes then shape the loaf and put it in the tin smooth side upwards. Cover it with oiled clingfilm again and leave for a further 30-40 minutes until the loaf has doubled in size. It's worth checking the dough regularly if you're using spelt flour, as I find it has a tendency to prove quickly.

Preheat the oven to 220°C/200°C fan/gas mark 7. Brush the top of the loaf with beaten egg then sprinkle with a handful of fennel seeds (or other seeds of your choice). Place the loaf on the upper middle shelf of the oven and bake for 15 minutes at 220°C/200°C fan/gas mark 7 before turning the heat down to 190°C/170°C fan/gas mark 5 and baking for a further 25-30 minutes. Tap the base of the loaf to hear whether it's hollow, which indicates that it's cooked through – it should also feel lighter than when it first went in the oven.

Leave in the tin for 10 minutes then turn out to cool on a wire rack.

The secret to making *smørbrød*

There is no gospel when it comes to Scandinavia's favourite lunchtime treat: the smørbrød *or open sandwich. You'll see that I have a particular bias towards* smørbrød *with seafood but there's no reason why you can't embellish your slice of rye, sourdough or farmhouse white bread with roast ham, beef, lamb, chicken or cheese. The trick is to mix colours, flavours and textures so that your open sandwich looks appetising and (more importantly) tastes delicious. Experiment with different combinations of toppings and garnishes, and why not try making your own oatmeal or spelt bread to be the perfect healthy base (pages 76 and 78, Lunch)? All of these* smørbrød *recipes can be also adapted to make quick and tasty canapes.*

Goat's cheese with radish and rosehip

Inspiration for this vegetarian topping came from a visit to Copenhagen where I ate rygeost, a delicious fresh cheese with a hint of smoke. It can be hard to find outside Denmark so I've improvised by adding a sprinkle of smoked sea salt to soft goat's cheese. The contrast between this and the sweet tang of the rosehip syrup, the crispiness of the radish and freshness of chervil works a treat. If you can't find rosehip syrup, try this with pomegranate syrup instead.

ENOUGH FOR 2

120g fresh spreadable goat's cheese
2 slices dark rye bread, pumpernickel or oatmeal bread
smoked sea salt
1-2 tbsp rosehip syrup
4-6 radishes, thinly sliced
chervil to garnish

Spread half the goat's cheese on each slice of rye bread and sprinkle with a small pinch of smoked sea salt. Taste the rosehip syrup – if it's very sweet use sparingly, but if it has a good hit of acidity, you may wish to use a little more than I've suggested. Drizzle the syrup on to the goat's cheese, and scatter radish slices and chervil leaves over the top of each *smørbrød*. Serve immediately.

Gravlaks and beetroot

As far as I'm concerned, Norwegian gravlaks — *known in Swedish as* gravadlax — *is quite possibly the best gourmet fast-food fish on the planet. Cured with dill, sea salt, sugar, coriander and white pepper for a few days, this Scandinavian classic is full of flavour yet delicate in texture, and utterly good for you. If you don't have the time or inclination to make your own (recipe on page 151, Dinner), then use a good quality local one. I think this tastes best with home-made sweet mustard sauce (page 151, Dinner) but I've given an alternative in case you fancy a speedier* smørbrød *snack. I love* gravlaks *as a quick lunch on sourdough crispbread, oatmeal bread or spelt and fennel seed bread (pages 76 and 78, Lunch), or with buttered new potatoes or even in a salad.*

SERVES 2

butter
4 small sourdough crispbread
4 generous slices *gravlaks*
4 tsp sweet mustard sauce, German mustard or crème fraiche
4 tbsp lightly pickled beetroot, chopped
dill to garnish
pinch of coriander seeds (optional)

Butter the crispbread then pile on the cured salmon, sweet mustard sauce and beetroot. Scatter dill fronds on top, add a few coriander seeds (if using) to pick up the coriander flavour in the gravlaks cure, and eat as soon as decently possible.

Mackerel, fennel and horseradish

Mackerel often gets overlooked, but it is a cheap and delicious fish, full of omega oils to nourish the brain and body. This rye bread sandwich is a great way to use up leftover grilled mackerel, but is also rather good with a lightly smoked fillet or mackerel tinned in olive oil. The idea of using fennel came from a visit to Aamann's *restaurant in Copenhagen, a top place for classic Danish* smørrebrød *with a modern twist. If you have one, use a mandolin slicer to shave the fennel in to paper-thin slices. If you can't find wood sorrel to garnish, just use fennel fronds on their own or mixed with chervil or parsley.*

SERVES 2

butter
2 slices dark rye bread or pumpernickel
2 tsp horseradish cream
1 large fillet cooked mackerel, de-boned
½ fennel bulb, thinly sliced
handful wood sorrel and fennel fronds,
  roughly shredded, to garnish

Butter the rye bread and then spread a thin layer of horseradish cream on each slice. Gently flake the mackerel on to the bread and top with the fennel slices. Garnish with wood sorrel and fennel fronds before serving.

Wild mushroom and tarragon

As we reach the end of summer, I start looking forward to the flavours and colours of autumn, and what better way to celebrate the change in the seasons than a simple dish where the autumnal wild mushroom is king? Chanterelles, morels, trompettes de la mort, porcini – all delicious with their own distinctive textures and flavours. This smørbrød *is perfect for lunch after a morning spent out foraging for mushrooms, but if picking your own doesn't appeal (or if you don't find any!), then you can always buy wild mushrooms or use chestnut mushrooms instead. This also makes a great speedy supper with the addition of a fried egg, or with some grated* Västerbotten *cheese sprinkled over the mushrooms and grilled until bubbling and golden.*

SERVES 2

2 large slices sourdough bread
1 garlic clove, peeled
butter for the toast, plus 1 tbsp for frying
1 tbsp vegetable oil
200g wild mushrooms and/or chestnut mushrooms
1 tsp sherry vinegar
1 sprig tarragon, chopped

Start by toasting the sourdough and, once toasted, rub the garlic clove enthusiastically over the surface of each slice to give it a good coating. Butter the garlicky toast and set aside on a wire rack to stop it going soggy, only transferring to plates just before you're ready to serve.

Heat the butter and vegetable oil in a frying pan. When the butter starts to foam, add the wild mushrooms and fry for 2 minutes until they've softened. Then add the sherry vinegar and chopped tarragon, and season with salt and pepper to taste.

Pile the fragrant mushrooms on top of the buttery garlicky toast and eat as soon as possible, while still piping hot.

Toast Skagen

*Toast Skagen is a classic open sandwich made with sweet North Sea prawns,
lumpfish roe, lemon, dill and mayonnaise. Skagen is a beautiful headland at the
northernmost tip of Denmark's Jutland peninsula where the North Sea and the Baltic
meet. It is a landscape covered with huge dunes, sandy beaches and picturesque little
red-tiled houses with yellow ochre walls. While Toast Skagen apparently originates from
this tiny corner of Denmark, it is available throughout Scandinavia and makes an
excellent brunch, lunch or starter. It is traditionally made with bread sautéed in butter,
but I prefer the healthier version using toast. If you don't fancy dill, substitute
parsley instead.*

SERVES 4

4 slices sourdough bread
mayonnaise
juice of ½ lemon
100g North Sea prawns, peeled
4 tsp lumpfish roe
4 thin slices lemon
small handful dill sprigs

Toast the sourdough and spread with as much or little mayonnaise as you like.
Sprinkle the lemon juice on to the mayonnaisey toast slices and then divide the
peeled prawns between them. Top each slice with a teaspoon of lumpfish roe,
a twisted lemon slice and a sprig or two of dill. Serve with a flourish.

Chopped egg and kaviar

The tube of Mills Kaviar, *block of* brunost *(Norwegian brown cheese) and jar of pickled herring that you will always find in my fridge are possibly the most consistent evidence of my Scandi roots. I find that they're great standbys for times when you're peckish but the supermarket's shut or you don't have time to cook. Eggs make the best standby of all as they're such a versatile partner to so many different foods and flavours. This sandwich is a family favourite, and I secretly relish the raised eyebrows that invariably result the first time that friends are offered 'caviar' from a tube... Actually,* Mills Kaviar *bears little relation to real caviar – it's a sweetly salty, lightly smoked pinky-orange cod roe – but I won't tell if you don't!*

SERVES 2

2 large slices sourdough bread
butter
Mills Kaviar
2 soft-boiled eggs, quartered
dill, roughly shredded (optional)

Toast and butter the sourdough and squeeze a decent amount of kaviar on to each slice. Traditionally you don't spread kaviar with a knife, so make sure that you squeeze it in a generous zig-zag or a few fat stripes, so that you'll have some in every bite. Then top each slice with four egg quarters and some chopped dill, if using. Eat immediately – the runny egg yolk tastes best while it's still hot.

Classic herring and potato

*I've been known to rant about how Scandinavian food isn't just herrings and
meatballs – but I confess that I do adore these classic dishes. I always keep a jar of herrings
in the fridge for a quick and easy light meal, and whenever I'm cooking new potatoes,
I boil extra so that I have them as a base for this sandwich the next day. The combination
of nutty rye bread, waxy potato slices, fragrant pickled herring and cool sour cream –
sheer Scandi heaven. If you don't have any herring fillets, 100g or so of rollmops works
just fine too.*

SERVES 2

butter
2 slices dark rye bread or pumpernickel
4 cooked and peeled new potatoes, sliced 0.5cm thin
2 large pickled herring fillets
2 tbsp sour cream
1 shallot, finely chopped
1 chive, finely chopped

Butter the rye bread and arrange the sliced new potatoes on top.
Lay a herring fillet on to each *smørbrød*, folding the ends of the fish over if
necessary so that it fits neatly on to its rye bread base. Dress each fillet with a
tablespoon of sour cream and a scattering of chopped shallot and chive,
and serve as soon as possible.

Chicken liver pâté with pickled beetroot

Scandinavians, from the southernmost Danish island of Bornholm in the Baltic to the northernmost tip of Norway (and in Iceland too), have a bit of a thing for liver pâté and fried onions. Traditional pork leverpostej *('liver paste') is served hot or cold, sliced or spread on rye bread with a topping of pickled gherkins, little sweet onions or beetroot. Fried golden brown crispy onions (*sprøstekt løk*) are available in every supermarket in little plastic tubs or bags and are put on everything from soups and salads to hotdogs, burgers and* smørbrød, *or even eaten on their own as a snack! This is my take on the traditional* smørbrød *using chicken pâté forestier on dark rye bread or home-made oatmeal bread (page 76, Lunch). I've given instructions here on how to make your own crispy onions, but do of course use Nordic pre-fried ones if you can get hold of them. Time-saving tip: if you make 3 or 4 times the quantity of fried onions needed for this recipe, you can store the remainder in an airtight container until you want them – they should keep for a few weeks.*

SERVES 2

1 medium onion, thinly sliced
1 tbsp oil
pinch of bicarbonate of soda
2 large slices dark rye bread, pumpernickel or oatmeal bread
170g chicken pâté forestier
sour cream
2 baby pickled beetroot, thinly sliced
chive blossom, chervil or parsley to garnish

Put the onion slices in the oil over a medium heat and once they start to sizzle, sprinkle with the bicarbonate of soda (it helps them to crisp up faster). Fry for 10-12 minutes until golden brown. Remove from the oil with a slotted spoon and place on a plate lined with kitchen paper to absorb any excess oil. Sprinkle with salt and allow to cool.

Spread the bread thickly with pâté, follow with a dollop of sour cream and arrange the slices of beetroot on top. Sprinkle with crispy onions and garnish with herbs or edible flowers. Admire for a moment before eating.

Crushed pea, bacon and tarragon

Happiness for me lies in the marriage of peas and bacon – a simple taste combination but utterly delicious, and one that can make you smile even on days when life throws you a curve ball. You need to be generous with the bacon on this sandwich, as the sweet peas need salty pork to bring out the very best in them. It would be remiss of me not to mention that crushed peas on toast also taste great as a vegetarian open sandwich with crumbled goat's cheese and a sprinkle of crispy onions (page 90, Lunch) or freshly sliced radish.

SERVES 2

150g smoked bacon lardons or streaky bacon
1 tbsp vegetable oil for frying
200g fresh or frozen peas
3 tbsp vegetable oil, bacon dripping or melted butter
1 tbsp lemon juice (or more to taste)
1 sprig tarragon
2 large slices white sourdough or crusty farmhouse bread
butter
coriander seeds (optional)

Fry the bacon in oil for 5 minutes or so over a medium heat, turning regularly. Once it is crispy and evenly cooked, remove from the pan and place on some kitchen paper to drain. Cook the peas in boiling water for 3 minutes until al dente, drain and then put in a blender with the oil (or dripping or butter, if using), lemon juice and tarragon. Season to taste with salt and pepper (and more lemon juice, if you feel it needs it). Toast the bread, spread with butter and generous layer of crushed peas and then heap on the crispy bacon. If you like a bit of extra crunch, sprinkle a few coriander seeds between the bacon bits to add a hint of spice.

Closed sandwiches

Much as I love the Scandinavian open sandwich, I firmly believe that there are some sandwiches that just have to be eaten closed. These two are my favourites, not only because they taste delicious but also because they are great ways to use up leftovers.

Nordic club sandwich

Being part-American, I have something of an obsession with club sandwiches. This is my Nordic version and frankly it's not a million miles away from what club sandwich purists would define as a true club. Anything goes, as long as it tastes good, I say. Besides, food rules are there to be broken. Except for the rule about using crunchy iceberg lettuce in a club – that's sacrosanct. I like to use big juicy slices of beef tomatoes (try Jack Hawkins variety), tangy Savora mustard, and a mix of light and dark allspice roast chicken leftovers (page 165, Dinner), but obviously you can vary these according to taste. Make sure you have all your ingredients prepared and to hand before you start putting everything together, as the key to a good club is making sure that the toast stays as crisp as possible. My other top tip for a beautifully stacked club is to hold it all together with a couple of strategically placed toothpicks, as otherwise everything tends to slither out sideways when you try to slice it or transport it a plate – but do make sure to remove them before eating!

SERVES 2

6-8 rashers smoked streaky bacon
6 slices wholemeal bread, thinly sliced
butter
2 tbsp Savora mustard
2 tbsp mayonnaise
130-150g cold roast chicken, sliced
6-8 slices *Jarlsberg* cheese
2 large beef tomatoes, thinly sliced
2 generous handfuls iceberg lettuce

Start by frying the bacon until it is good and crispy. Once cooked, remove from the heat and pop it on some kitchen paper to cool. Toast the bread, then butter each piece and add a layer of Savora mustard and mayonnaise. Place one piece of toast on each plate (or share a large plate and save on washing up) and start piling up a layer of each of: roast chicken, bacon rashers, *Jarlsberg*, tomato and iceberg lettuce. Cover with another slice of toast (mustardy mayonnaise side upwards) and repeat the layering process, before topping each one with a final slice of toast (mayonnaise side downwards this time!) Carefully press together and hold it all in place with a couple of toothpicks pushed through the full depth of each double-decker sandwich. Very gently slice each club in half, either straight through the middle in rectangles or diagonally in traditional triangles, as the mood takes you. Eat straight away.

Meatball baguette

In my family meatball sandwiches are always eaten the day after a meatball bonanza dinner – in fact we always cook more meatballs than we need, in order to make sure that there are enough left over (page 168, Dinner). Although it may not sound like the most refined Scandinavian cuisine, let me assure you that this is the sandwich of champions. Cold meatballs taste simply fantastic on buttered bread with a wodge of lingonberry jam or a squirt of tomato ketchup.

This is an updated version of the traditional meatball smørbrød. Over the years I've come round to the idea of covering them with a second layer of bread, and even though I am generally a wholemeal bread fan, meatballs definitely taste best sandwiched along the length of a crusty white baguette.

SERVES 2

1 long white baguette
butter
lingonberry jam (or tomato ketchup)
2 handfuls lettuce leaves
16 cold meatballs

Slice the baguette in half lengthways and spread each open face with butter and a layer of lingonberry jam. Lay a bed of lettuce leaves on the bottom half of the baguette and then arrange the meatballs down its length. Sandwich the two halves of the baguette firmly together and slice in the middle to make two chunky sandwiches. To eat, forget all semblance of table manners, grasp with both hands, open wide and sink your teeth in to the baguette. Ideally, chase down with a glass of chilled beer.

Roasted swede soup

Imported to England from Sweden and originally called a swedish turnip, the swede tends to be much maligned outside Scandinavia. The mere mention of swede (also known as rutabaga, from the Swedish rotabagge) often evokes unwelcome memories of watery overboiled school dinners. But those who dismiss this versatile root vegetable out of hand are really missing a trick. Swede mashes beautifully with carrot and potato or parsnip, and roasting it brings out its inherent sweetness. The sour cream in this recipe gives a nice tart contrast to this sweetness, but use double cream if you prefer a less assertive flavour. It is worth making a large batch of this soup and freezing some for those days when you don't feel like cooking. This soup goes brilliantly with spelt and fennel bread (page 78, Lunch) or Jarlsberg and fennel muffins (page 63, Brunch).

SERVES 6-8

2 heads swede, peeled and chopped into large chunks
4-5 tbsp vegetable oil
2 onions, finely chopped
2 celery sticks, finely chopped
2 large carrots, peeled and finely chopped
2 tbsp vegetable oil
2 tbsp butter
whole nutmeg, for grating
1½ litres hot vegetable stock
300ml sour cream
chervil, chive blossom or finely chopped parsley or chive to garnish (optional)

Preheat the oven to 200°C/180°C fan/gas mark 6.

Place the chopped swede in a large roasting tin, drizzle with oil, season with salt and a sprinkle of freshly ground white pepper and roast in the oven for 35-45 minutes until the swede is soft and slightly browned.

Sweat the onion, celery and carrot in the vegetable oil and butter in a large saucepan over a low heat for 5 minutes until the onion is soft and translucent. Grate in half a nutmeg, then add the roasted swede and hot vegetable stock. Simmer for 15-20 minutes and then blitz with a handheld blender or in a heatproof glass blender until smooth. If you're using an upright liquidiser, do make sure that the lid is securely on – I keep a tea towel pressed firmly on top just to make sure that the soup doesn't erupt and force the lid off when I start blending. Season to taste and then return to the pan to keep warm.

Serve in large bowls and top with a dollop of sour cream in the middle of each, followed by a grating or two of nutmeg and a sprinkle of chopped herbs (if using) to finish with a flourish.

Mama Johansen's vegetable soup

My mother possesses the marvellous and somewhat underrated talent of knowing precisely what to do with leftover vegetables after a big meal. More often than not, I find that the best solution is soup. This one is satisfying and virtuous in equal measure, perfect for chilly days when salads or sandwiches don't quite cut the mustard. You can use raw or cooked vegetables for this soup – if the onion and leek are already cooked then you don't need to sweat them down, and if the other soup veggies are also pre-cooked, then you can reduce the simmering time to 2-3 minutes before blitzing. I've suggested using leek, potato, broccoli and asparagus, but you could use carrot, cauliflower, swede, parsnip, peas, jerusalem artichoke, kohlrabi, beetroot, sweet potato or any other vegetable that takes your fancy – soup doesn't have to be green to be tasty!

SERVES 4

1 banana shallot, finely chopped
1 leek, finely chopped
2 tbsp vegetable oil
8 medium new potatoes, cooked and peeled
½ head raw broccoli, roughly chopped
4 raw asparagus spears, roughly chopped
300-400ml vegetable stock
crème fraiche or sour cream (optional)

Sweat the shallot and leek in the vegetable oil in a medium saucepan over a low heat for 5 minutes until soft and translucent. Add the potatoes, broccoli, asparagus and vegetable stock, stir and bring to a gentle simmer for 8-10 minutes.

Whizz the soup up with a handheld blender or in a heatproof glass blender (keeping a firm hand and a tea towel on the liquidiser lid to avoid any soup explosions during blending). Season to taste with salt and freshly ground white pepper and return to the pan to reheat. Serve piping hot in large bowls just as it is, or with a dollop of crème fraiche or sour cream swirled in.

Cream of tomato and cardamom soup

Cream of tomato soup may not seem particularly Scandinavian but it was something my Norwegian grandmother would make for us on cold winter afternoons, adding cooked macaroni to the soup shortly before serving if we were well behaved. I adored it and still find myself craving tomato soup when the weather gets frosty. If you have any leftover meatballs not destined for sandwiches (page 94, Lunch; page 168, Dinner) pop them in the soup to heat through for a few minutes before serving, as they go extremely well with the creamy tomato.

The cardamom adds a fragrant twist to an otherwise simple dish, but if you prefer, you can use other spices instead – coriander, fennel seed, juniper berry or star anise would work well with tomatoes. The coconut cream not only balances the acidity of the tomatoes but also provides another layer of flavour. It's a great subsitute if you are avoiding dairy, but of course if you're not keen on coconut then simply use double cream. This soup is, as the name would suggest, already quite creamy, but if you fancy making it even more luxurious, you could swirl a little crème fraiche or Greek yoghurt through just before serving.

SERVES 4

1 onion, finely chopped
1 tbsp oil
1 tbsp butter
1 tsp freshly ground cardamom
2 tins chopped tomatoes
160ml tin coconut cream
300ml hot vegetable stock
dill, chervil or roughly chopped parsley to garnish (optional)

Sweat the onion in the oil and butter in a medium saucepan over a low heat for 5-7 minutes until soft and translucent. Add the cardamom and fry for a further minute.

Next add the tomatoes and coconut cream. This will initially make the soup alarmingly pink but it gradually turns to the more familiar orange-red colour during the cooking process. Add the hot stock, stir through and simmer on the hob over a low-medium heat for 15-20 minutes.

Blitz with a handheld blender or in a heatproof glass standing blender – if using a standing liquidiser, I tend to hold a tea towel firmly over the lid to avoid decorating myself and my kitchen with hot tomato soup as it blitzes. Season to taste and then return to the pan to reheat before serving with a garnish of herbs (if using) and a chunk of good crusty bread or baguette to accompany.

Tangy egg and potato salad

This is a pepped-up version of a traditional Scandinavian dill, egg and potato salad.
This salad tastes great just as it is, or try it with cold cooked salmon, smoked trout, leftover
roast beef or roast ham instead of (or, if you're hungry, in addition to) the egg. I prefer to
use German gherkins for this salad when I can get hold of them as they're not too salty.

SERVES 4

400g baby new potatoes, washed
4 spring onions, thinly sliced
2 shallots, finely chopped
2 large gherkins, finely chopped
200ml sour cream
1 heaped tbsp salad cream
1-2 tbsp grainy mustard
4 sprigs dill, finely chopped, plus 1 extra to garnish
juice of ½ lemon
pinch of freshly ground allspice
4 hard-boiled eggs, shelled and quartered

Put the new potatoes in a medium saucepan, cover with boiling water, add a pinch
of salt and simmer gently for 10-15 minutes until they're cooked through. Test one
with a fork to see that it goes through smoothly while the potato remains whole –
you don't want to overcook the potatoes or they'll lose their firm texture and become
mushy in the salad. Drain the potatoes in a colander and allow to cool near an open
window for 15 minutes or so while you prepare the dressing.

Put the spring onion, shallots, gherkins, sour cream, salad cream, mustard, dill,
lemon juice and allspice in a medium bowl, mix and season to taste. It should be
creamily tart and tangy, allowing you to identify all the individual flavours.

When the potatoes have cooled to room temperature, toss them in the dressing and
serve in a large salad bowl, topped with the quartered eggs and garnished with a
small sprig of dill.

Crunchy salad with lemon and mustard

This flavourful salad is similar to coleslaw but with rather more punch, courtesy of the mustard and horseradish. It uses kohlrabi which is a rather underrated vegetable, but which I like for its refreshing radish-like crunch and mildly cauliflowery flavour. It is a great dish for days when you fancy a salad, but know that delicate little lettuce leaves won't be enough to sustain you for an afternoon's hard graft. It works very well as an accompaniment to barbecued fish, meat or chicken or oven-baked potatoes. If you have any edible flowers – violets, borage, primrose, marigold, chamomile, cowslip or nasturtium – then a handful of these scattered on the top just before serving looks stunning.

SERVES 4-6

1 white or red cabbage

1 large kohlrabi, peeled

4 large carrots, peeled

2 eating apples, cored

2 bulbs fennel, including fronds
  to garnish

300ml sour cream

juice of ½ lemon

1-2 tbsp grainy mustard

1 tsp horseradish cream

1 tsp fennel seeds, crushed

½ tsp coriander seeds, crushed

Start by trimming any battered or unappetising-looking outer leaves from the cabbage, then quartering it and cutting out the tough interior. Slice the cabbage, kohlrabi, carrots and apples in to thin shreds of roughly the same size using a mandoline slicer or a good sharp knife. Remove the fennel fronds and set aside for the garnish. Slice the fennel as thinly as you can, ideally 2mm thick or so – this will be a lot easier if you are using a mandoline. Put all the sliced ingredients together in a large bowl.

Whisk or fork together all the remaining ingredients in a small bowl to make the dressing. Season to taste. It should have a pleasingly sour citrussy tang, but if it's too acidic for your taste, then add a pinch of sugar and a good couple of pinches of salt. Pour the dressing over the sliced ingredients and mix well. The easiest way to distribute it is to use your hands and squelch it all together, so that there's a coating of sour cream dressing on everything.

Refrigerate for 30 minutes to let the flavours infuse, then serve with a garnish of fennel fronds and, if you have any, a cheery scattering of edible flowers.

Egg, beetroot and cottage cheese salad

Cottage cheese goes in and out of fashion, and is frequently referred to rather disparagingly as 'diet food'. This seems a shame as it's really rather good, and has just the right amount of salt and creaminess to make a tasty base for a quick salad. My mother used to make this salad for me when I was growing up. Nowadays we tend to prepare it together, but it's just as delicious as it was back then. You can use any salad leaves for this, so be as adventurous as you like – try mixing dandelion, rocket, watercress, baby spinach and beetroot leaves – or keep it simple with crunchy cos, romaine or iceberg if you prefer.

SERVES 2

4 pickled beetroots
¼ cucumber
2 handfuls salad leaves
250g plain cottage cheese
6-10 ripe cherry tomatoes
2 hardboiled eggs, cooled and shelled
oil and vinegar to dress

Cut the beetroots into quarters or eighths, depending on how big they are and how chunky you like your salad to be. Quarter the cucumber lengthways into sticks and then slice in to bite-sized chunks.

Put a couple of handfuls of salad leaves on two plates and arrange half the cottage cheese, tomatoes, beetroot and cucumber on each one, spreading it out to cover the salad base or piling it high in the middle, as the mood takes you.

Quarter the eggs and divide between the plates. Season with salt and pepper and drizzle with oil and vinegar. Serve on its own or with a few slices of dark rye, sourdough, oatmeal or spelt and fennel seed bread.

Hot smoked trout salad

One of my favourite summer dishes, this hot smoked trout salad is fresh, light and full of flavour. Use whatever salad leaves take your fancy – little gem, cos, lollo rosso, baby spinach, watercress, dandelion and beetroot leaves or whatever else you have handy! If you can't find hot smoked trout then simply substitute hot smoked salmon or mackerel, or cold cooked salmon instead. Try this recipe with raspberry or cider vinegar if you can't find apple vinegar with lingonberries.

SERVES 4

4 fillets hot smoked trout
1 tbsp horseradish sauce
4 tbsp apple vinegar with lingonberries
7 tbsp rapeseed or sunflower oil
1 head lettuce or c.150-200g mixed salad leaves, washed and roughly shredded
4 sprigs mint, finely shredded
2 shallots, finely chopped
½ cucumber, thinly sliced or shredded
8 radishes, thinly sliced

Start by shredding the trout into bite-size pieces on a small plate. Next make the vinaigrette: use a fork to whisk together the horseradish and the vinegar in a small bowl, then slowly pour in the oil, whisking all the while to emulsify the dressing. Season to taste with salt and pepper.

Put the lettuce, mint and shallots with the vinaigrette in a large bowl and toss well to ensure that all the leaves are dressed. Divide the salad between four plates, scatter the cucumber and radish slices over the leaves, and top each plate with a quarter of the hot smoked trout pieces. Enjoy as a light meal on its own or accompanied by sourdough crispbread or thinly sliced and toasted dark rye bread, oatmeal bread or spelt and fennel seed bread (pages 76 and 78, Lunch).

Afternoon Cake

Fika and *hygge* are time-honoured, quintessentially Scandinavian concepts. *Fika* is a Swedish word used for a get-together with friends for a chat over a cup of coffee and something sweet, whereas the Norwegian/Danish *hygge* is more general, and roughly equates to celebrating friends, family and conviviality – often with food, drink and cosy candlelight to banish the gloom on long dark winter evenings. And what better way to celebrate the good things in life than to sit down together in the afternoon with a cup of something warming and a home-baked treat to keep it company?

You could try something different from the usual tea or coffee: a steaming mugful of hot fruit cordial works wonders to banish the chills on cool autumn days, zesty spiced *gløgg* is perfect for Christmas parties and my chocoholic hot chocolate shot can help overcome even the sleepiest of mid-afternoon slumps.

As for what to have with it, well, a slice of delicately spiced apple cake, buttery caramelised coconut sponge or rich chocolatey indulgence is always divine. If cakes aren't your thing, try little lemony choux buns or marzipan and vanilla cream-filled cardamom buns, a Lenten treat across Scandinavia. Or why not make your own gifts for family and friends by baking saffron choc chip biscotti and cloud-like coconut macaroons. They keep well and everyone loves a home-made treat!

Hot chocolate shot
Spiced blueberry juice
Scandilicious *gløgg*
Spiced apple cake
Blackberry, almond and cardamom cake
Mor Monsen (Norwegian lemon, currant and almond cake)
Drømmekage (Danish coconut dream cake)
Tropisk aroma (Norwegian spiced chocolate cake)
Kladdkaka (Swedish gooey chocolate cake)
Daim cake
Mustikkapiirakka (Finnish blueberry tart)
Mama Johansen's plum muffins
Chocolate mocha coconut muffins
Saffransskorpor (Swedish saffron and choc chip biscuits)
Kokosmakroner (Norwegian coconut macaroons)
Lemony choux buns
Fastelavensboller or *semlor*
   (Scandinavian cardamom cream buns)

Hot chocolate shot

Being a confirmed chocoholic, I like to try the local hot chocolate wherever I go.
The best I ever tasted was in Milan, but since that's rather a long way to go for a hot
drink, this is my version. It is best served in espresso or small tea cups as it's intended as
an intensely chocolatey shot rather than a milky mugful. For flavour variations, try
adding a splash of vanilla extract or a little freshly ground cardamom or grated nutmeg.

SERVES 1

25g dark chocolate or pure cacao
50-75ml water
pinch of sea salt
light brown muscovado sugar or maple syrup to taste

Put the chocolate, water and salt in a small saucepan over a medium heat and whisk
while you bring to the boil. Simmer for 3-4 minutes or until it looks molten and viscous.
Sweeten to taste – you'll need more sugar if you're using pure cacao than if you're
using chocolate. Pour into a little cup and enjoy while it's steaming hot. Any left over
can be reheated later to drink, or used as chocolate sauce.

Spiced blueberry juice

In autumn and winter, I find that hot juice or cordial makes a refreshing change from the usual tea and coffee, and the fruit sugars really hit the spot when you need a sweet treat. It is particularly restorative if you're feeling sniffly, as it gives you a reviving boost of vitamin C and warming spices. For a little variety, why not try other juices or cordials? Pomegranate, apple, blackcurrant, cranberry, lingonberry, elderflower and rosehip all work wonderfully.

SERVES 2

500ml blueberry juice (or high fruit cordial diluted to taste)
4 cloves
2 star anise
2 cardamom pods
1 cinnamon stick
1 small knob of fresh ginger (optional)
juice of ½ lemon
2 lemon slices to serve

Put the blueberry juice and dried spices in a saucepan. If using, cut the knob of ginger in two, bash it to 'bruise' it and release the juice, and place in the pan with the blueberry juice. Bring the mixture to a gentle boil and simmer for 10 minutes. Remove the ginger pieces and strain the hot liquid in to two mugs using a tea strainer to remove the spices. Pour half the lemon juice in each mug and float a slice of lemon on top for good measure before serving.

Scandilicious *gløgg*

Gløgg is Scandinavia's yuletide take on mulled wine or Glühwein. *Traditionally you drink gløgg with raisins and skinned almonds in it, but I use dried sour cherries soaked in cherry liqueur instead of raisins, and have been known to substitute unsalted shelled pistachios for the almonds. There are no hard and fast rules, so use whatever fruit and nut combination takes your fancy, or leave them out altogether if you prefer. I tend to use a full-bodied red wine like a Bordeaux for this recipe. You could make white gløgg by using a dry white wine instead of red, and using Grand Marnier, aquavit or brandy in place of cherry liqueur to soak the dried fruit.*

The spiced sugar syrup should ideally be prepared a day in advance to allow plenty of time for the spices to infuse, but if you don't get the chance, just make sure that it has about an hour or so to infuse on the day that you're going to use it. It's a very versatile syrup that tastes great in fruit salads and hot drinks, so you may wish to make double quantities and store the unused portion in a sterilised jam jar or screw-top bottle in the fridge for up to a month.

SERVES 8

1cm knob of fresh ginger	100g dried sour cherries
75g fructose (or 115g caster sugar)	100ml cherry liqueur
8 whole cloves	750ml bottle red wine
8 cardamom pods, crushed	50ml cherry liqueur
3 star anise	80g skinned almonds
2 cinnamon sticks	1 unwaxed (or well-scrubbed waxed)
5cm long paring of lemon zest	orange (optional)

THE NIGHT BEFORE / AN HOUR OR SO BEFORE MAKING THE *GLØGG*

Cut the knob of ginger in two, bash it to 'bruise' it and release the juice. Bring the fructose, fresh ginger, dried spices, piece of lemon rind and 200ml of water to a simmer in a small saucepan. As soon as the fructose has fully dissolved, turn off the heat, cover and set the spiced sugar syrup aside to infuse. Put the dried cherries in 100ml of cherry liqueur, cover and leave to soak.

ON THE DAY

Strain the sugar syrup to remove the spices. Simmer the syrup and red wine in a large saucepan for 5 minutes – don't boil it any more vigorously than this as otherwise all the alcohol will evaporate! Add 50ml of cherry liqueur for extra flavour and simmer for another minute. Put a small handful of skinned almonds and boozy cherries in heatproof glasses or cups and pour the *gløgg* over them. As a finishing flourish, if you fancy it, garnish each drink with a thin slice of orange, or peel zest strips from the orange with a vegetable peeler, twist a small slice of orange zest over each drink and run the twisted zest along the rim of each mug or glass for an extra hint of citrus as you drink.

Spiced apple cake

My family loves cooked apples in all their guises: cake, crumble, strudel, pie... you name it. Sometimes the best cakes are the ones invented on the spur of the moment. This one came into being one day when I felt like baking using whatever ingredients I had to hand – and this was the delicious result. A perfect mid-afternoon autumnal treat, complete with the soothing scent of spices and cooked apples. I like the tartness of the cooking apple on top of the sweet cake, or try it with plums or apricots for a jammier version. You can of course use a mixture of plain and wholemeal wheat flour rather than spelt, if you prefer.

SERVES 8-10

150g butter, softened
250g light brown
  muscovado sugar
2 medium eggs
150g refined spelt flour
50g wholemeal spelt flour
50g ground almonds
2 tsp baking powder

⅛ tsp bicarbonate of soda
1 tsp cinnamon, plus more to top
½ tsp cardamom
¼ tsp nutmeg
¼ tsp salt
100ml sour cream
1 large cooking apple, peeled
  and sliced into thin slivers

Preheat the oven to 180°C/160°C fan/gas mark 4 and lightly oil a 22cm round cake tin.

Cream the butter and sugar together in a large bowl until pale and fluffy. Mix in the eggs along with two tablespoons of the refined spelt flour to prevent the mixture from curdling. Sift the rest of the flour (both types) with the ground almonds, raising agents, spices and salt in to a medium bowl.

Whisk the sour cream in to the butter mixture, then stir in the sifted dry ingredients using a large metal spoon to make figure-of-eights in the mixture until it is fully combined. Pour the batter into the cake tin and top with the apple slices – you can arrange them in a pattern or simply scatter them randomly, as I do. Sprinkle a bit more cinnamon over the apples and then put the cake on the middle shelf of the oven and bake for 30-35 minutes until golden-brown and firm to the touch. You can test it by inserting a skewer – if it comes out cleanly or with only a trace of crumbs on it, then the cake is done.

Leave to cool in its tin on a wire rack for 10 minutes or so before turning out – although you don't have to wait until it's completely cool if, like me, you can't resist the smell, as this cake tastes fabulous eaten while still warm. Serve just as it is or with an indulgent dollop of sour cream. This cake keeps for 2-3 days if kept in an airtight container.

Blackberry, almond and cardamom cake

Simple, sweet and delicious, this cardamom-scented almond cake works just as well with other fruit. Try it with raspberries, blackcurrants, cherries or even little plums for a lovely gluten-free afternoon treat.

SERVES 6-8

125g butter, softened
200g golden caster sugar
1 tsp vanilla extract
3 medium eggs
250g ground almonds
2 tsp gluten-free baking powder
1 tsp ground cardamom
¼ tsp salt
200g fresh or frozen blackberries
200g summer berries to serve (optional)

Preheat the oven to 180°C/160°C fan/gas mark 4 and lightly oil a 23cm round cake tin.

Cream the butter, sugar and vanilla extract together in a large bowl until pale and fluffy. Add the eggs one at a time along with a tablespoonful of ground almonds to stop the mixture splitting.

Mix the rest of the ground almonds with the baking powder, ground cardamom and salt in a medium bowl, and then use a large metal spoon to fold these dry ingredients in to the butter mixture. Stir until just blended, add the blackberries and stir once or twice more to incorporate them. Scoop the cake mixture into the prepared tin and bake on the middle oven shelf for 30-35 minutes or until the cake has risen, looks golden brown and feels firm to the touch.

Cool in its tin on a wire rack before turning out. Serve this cake either on its own or with mixed summer fruits piled on top and with some sour cream or crème fraiche. This is quite a moist cake, so it will keep for 3-4 days in an airtight tin or wrapped in foil.

Mor Monsen
(Norwegian lemon, currant and almond cake)

No one seems to know who Mother Monsen was, but every good Norwegian knows her fruity buttery cake. My Norwegian grandmother always seemed to have a tin full of it in the kitchen. It goes well with a cup of good coffee but even better with a pot of Earl Grey, Lady Grey or fruity Oolong tea to complement its citrus and almond flavours. If you can't find unwaxed lemons, just give a regular one a good wash and scrub to remove any wax from the peel.

MAKES 12-16 SLICES

250g butter, softened
250g golden caster sugar
1 tsp vanilla extract
3 medium eggs, separated
200g refined spelt
 (or plain) flour
zest and juice of 1 unwaxed lemon
75g ground almonds

2 tsp baking powder
1/8 tsp bicarbonate of soda
1/4 tsp sea salt
75g currants, soaked in water
 for 10 minutes
pinch of salt
40g toasted slivers of almonds
4-5 tbsp natural sugar crystals

Preheat the oven to 180°C/160°C fan/gas mark 4. Lightly oil a 20 x 30cm rectangular cake tin and set aside.

Cream the butter, sugar and vanilla extract together in a large bowl until light and fluffy. Mix in the egg yolks one at a time along with a tablespoon of flour each time to keep the mixture from splitting. Add the lemon zest and juice along with the rest of the flour, ground almonds, baking powder, bicarbonate of soda and sea salt, and use a large spoon to fold them in to the butter mixture until evenly combined. Drain the currants and fold them in too.

Whisk the egg whites in a separate bowl with a pinch of salt until they reach stiff peaks. You'll find this easier if the egg whites are at room temperature. Add one-third of the beaten whites to the cake batter and fold through to loosen the mixture. Then fold in the rest of the egg whites, using figure-of-eight motions so that you retain as much air as possible. Don't worry if there's the odd bit of egg white still showing – it's better to keep the mixture light and you can always blend them in with a small teaspoon or a toothpick.

Carefully scoop the mixture in to the cake tin and scatter the almonds and sugar crystals on top before baking on the middle shelf of the oven for 20-25 minutes until golden yellow and firm to the touch. Remove from the oven and allow to cool in its tin by an open window before cutting diagonally into diamond-shaped pieces. This cake keeps well in a tin or sealed container for 3-4 days.

Drømmekage
(Danish coconut dream cake)

Being nearly as addicted to coconut as I am to cardamom and cinnamon, drømmekage *or 'dream cake' was a blissful discovery at* Lagkagehuset, *one of Copenhagen's fabulous bakeries. Dream cake is exactly that, as far as I am concerned: a sweet buttery sponge cake topped with caramelised coconut that somehow manages to be simultaneously crispy and chewy. I've given a few alternative topping suggestions if you're not much of a coconut fan. If you can't get hold of buttermilk, use 150ml of milk with a teaspoon of lemon juice in it to acidify it; and if you can't find vanilla salt in the shops, you can make it very simply by combining vanilla pod seeds with sea salt (one pod is enough for about 225g salt), which can then be stored in an airtight jar with the scraped pod for extra flavour.*

MAKES 12 GENEROUS OR 16 MODEST SLICES

4 medium eggs
300g golden caster sugar
1 tsp vanilla extract
150g butter, melted
150ml buttermilk
300g refined spelt (or plain) flour
3 tsp baking powder
¼ tsp salt
Topping
200g butter
200g light brown soft sugar
150g desiccated coconut
100ml whole milk
1 heaped tsp vanilla sea salt

Preheat the oven to 190°C/170°C fan/gas mark 5. Lay two sheets of parchment paper over each other at 90° to form a cross in the base of a 20cm x 30cm rectangular cake tin – this makes it easier to remove the cake when baked.

Whisk the eggs, sugar and vanilla with an electric mixer in a large bowl until pale. When you lift the electric beaters, a ribbon of mixture should hang from them for 2-3 seconds before dropping.

Pour in half the melted butter and buttermilk, and then sift in half the flour. Using a large metal spoon, slice through the mixture in swift figure-of-eight movements to incorporate as much flour, butter and buttermilk in as quickly as possible without knocking out all the air from the whisked eggs.

Now pour the rest of the butter and buttermilk in, and sift in the rest of the flour along with the baking powder and salt. Stir through using the same figure-of-eight motion from the bottom of the bowl to the top. It's not a crisis if a few blobs of flour surface – as long as the mixture looks evenly mixed then you're good to go.

Pour the batter into the prepared cake tin and bake on the middle shelf of the oven for 20 minutes or until the cake has doubled in size, looks golden-caramel in colour and feels firm to the touch. Insert a skewer if you're uncertain: there should be no uncooked mixture remaining on the skewer when you pull it out.

While the cake is cooking, prepare the coconut mixture by heaping all the topping ingredients in a medium saucepan and bringing to a simmer while stirring continuously so the sugar doesn't scorch on the bottom of the pan. Cook for 5 minutes until the mixture looks thick and some of the liquid has evaporated. You don't want it to be too wet as a topping for the cake. Taste to check the seasoning – vanilla sea salt really lifts the flavour so don't scrimp on the salt if you feel it needs a little more!

Once you have removed the cake from the oven, turn the heat up to 220°C/200°C fan/ gas mark 7. Use a spatula to spread the coconut mixture gently over the surface of the cake so that it gets an even coating, but taking care not to squash it down completely. Return the coconut-covered cake to the oven and place on the upper-middle shelf this time. Bake for a further 5-10 minutes, keeping an eye on the topping which should change colour from a pale caramel to a toasted, deep golden colour. Don't let it bake for too long or the sugar will start to go black and will taste acrid.

Remove from the oven and cool in its tin near an open window. Eat with dreamy pleasure. This cake will keep for several days if stored in an airtight container.

TOPPING VARIATIONS

* For nut-lovers, try making it into *Toscakake* by substituting toasted and finely chopped almonds or hazelnuts for the desiccated coconut in the gooey topping.

* For chocolate-coffee caramel *Bømlokake*, replace the milk in the topping with one shot of good espresso, 1 tablespoon of cocoa powder and 50g of dark chocolate, broken into pieces. If you like a very intense chocolate flavour, increase the quantity to 75g-100g dark chocolate.

* You could combine the previous suggestions, replacing the milk and coconut in the dream cake topping recipe with espresso, cocoa, dark chocolate and toasted nuts (quantities as above).

Tropisk aroma
(Norwegian spiced chocolate cake)

*Scandinavians seem to love the combination of chocolate and spices – possibly something
we picked up from our Germanic neighbours to the south who are famous for their
Christmas gingerbread and* Lebkuchen. *This marbled cake is always a staple at my family's
birthdays, weddings and special occasions, but don't save it for high days and holidays.
A generous slice of* tropisk aroma *is divine with a cup of really good coffee any time...*

SERVES 8-10

150g butter, softened
250g golden caster sugar
2 medium eggs
250g self-raising flour
1 tsp grated nutmeg
1 tsp cinnamon
pinch of salt
120ml whole milk
2 tbsp plain yoghurt

1 tbsp strong coffee or espresso
2 tbsp cocoa powder
Frosting
200g butter, softened
200g icing sugar
2 tsp coffee powder
4 tbsp cocoa powder, plus more
   to finish (optional)
1 tsp vanilla extract

Preheat oven to 180°C/160°C fan/gas mark 4. Lightly oil 23cm round cake tin and fit
the bottom with baking parchment.

Cream the butter and sugar together in a large bowl until pale and then add the eggs one at
a time, whisking each one in thoroughly, along with a tablespoon of the flour each time to
prevent the mixture splitting, before adding the next egg. Mix the rest of the flour, the spices
and a pinch of salt in a medium bowl. Mix together the milk, yoghurt and coffee in a jug.
Stir about a third of the flour mix in to the butter mixture and then stir in one-third of the
liquids, alternating until everything has been incorporated and you have a thick cake batter.

Put one-third of the batter in a smaller bowl, add the cocoa powder and stir thoroughly.

Pour half the plain batter in to the bottom of the cake tin, then pour the chocolate batter
on top. Cover with the remaining half of the plain mixture and use a fork to swirl through
the layers to create a marbled effect. Bake on the middle shelf of the oven for 35-40 minutes
until a skewer inserted in the middle comes out clean of any cake mix.

Remove the cake from its tin after 10 minutes or so and leave to cool on a wire rack while
you make the frosting by creaming the butter with the icing sugar, the coffee and cocoa
powders and the vanilla extract in a medium bowl.

When the cake is completely cool, spread the icing all over the top and sides. Sprinkle
with a little extra cocoa powder if you fancy a double cocoa hit. You can keep this cake for
2-3 days in an airtight container. It also freezes remarkably well (frosted or unfrosted).

Kladdkaka
(Swedish gooey chocolate cake)

Kladdkaka – *literally 'gooey cake' – is a dense sticky chocolate cake. This is my friend Christina's brilliant bona fide Swedish recipe for* kladdkaka. *It's ideal for that late afternoon slump when you really, really need some chocolate, or you could even serve it as a delicious way to round off a dinner party. If you want to make gluten-free* kladdkaka, *simply substitute ground almonds for the flour.*

SERVES 8-10

200g dark chocolate
200g unsalted butter, cubed
4 large eggs
200g caster sugar
250g plain flour
1 tsp baking powder

Preheat the oven to 220°C/200°C fan/gas mark 7. Lightly oil a loose-bottomed 23cm round cake tin.

Break the chocolate in to small pieces. Melt the butter over a medium heat in a small saucepan and then remove from the heat. Add the chocolate to the melted butter in the hot pan, stir until the chocolate melts and then leave to cool. Whisk the eggs and sugar in a large bowl until pale and fluffy, then stir in the cooled (but still fluid) chocolate mixture.

Carefully fold in the flour and baking powder, trying not to lose too much of the air from the whisked eggs. Pour the batter in to the tin and bake on the middle shelf of the oven for 12-13 mins. Do not be tempted to bake for longer or it will overcook – the aim is to end up with something like a gooey chocolate brownie, not dry cake.

Cool in its tin. Once cooled, it can be stored in an airtight container for 3-4 days. Serve with lightly whipped cream spiked with vanilla or a splash of Grand Marnier.

Daim cake

Daim bars, originally called Dime in the UK, are made of chocolate-covered crunchy almond brittle and are hugely popular in Scandinavia. The combination of creamy milk chocolate and buttery krokan makes a perfect base for chocolate cake, and this flour-free recipe is a big favourite with kids and adults alike. If you can't get hold of Daim bars, then use ordinary milk chocolate instead. The surprise ingredient is brunost, the Norwegian brown cheese. I think it adds an extra dimension to this cake, giving it a subtle sweet-savoury taste similar to salted caramel. However, if you can't find it or don't fancy it, simply substitute additional milk chocolate instead.

SERVES 6-8

75g milk chocolate with
Daim (or chopped up
Daim bar)
50g butter
75g *brunost*
200g ground almonds
2 tbsp cocoa

1 tsp baking powder
pinch of salt
3 medium eggs
200g icing sugar
1 tsp vanilla extract
Topping
100g milk chocolate

with *Daim* (or chopped
up *Daim* bar)
50g butter or coconut oil
1 tbsp cocoa
¼ tsp vanilla extract
1 pack of *Daim* balls

Preheat the oven to 180°C/160°C fan/gas mark 4. Lightly oil a deep 20cm round cake tin and set aside.

Put the milk chocolate, butter and *brunost* in a heatproof bowl over a saucepan containing a couple of centimetres of simmering water and melt together until smooth. Remove the bowl from the heat and allow to cool. Mix the ground almonds, cocoa, baking powder and a pinch of salt in a medium bowl. In a separate bowl, whisk the eggs, icing sugar and vanilla extract until pale and fluffy.

Carefully pour the melted chocolate in to the egg mixture, stir a couple of times and then add the dry ingredients, folding through 6-8 times with a large metal spoon until the mixture looks even. Pour the cake batter in to the tin and bake on the middle shelf of the oven for 20-25 minutes until the top looks golden brown and feels firm to the touch, and the cake starts to separate from the sides of the cake tin.

Remove the cake from the oven and leave to cool in its tin while you prepare the topping. Melt the milk chocolate and butter (or oil) together in a heatproof bowl resting on top of a saucepan containing a couple of centimetres of simmering water, and then stir in the cocoa and vanilla. While the topping is still warm, pierce the cake a dozen or so times with a skewer and spread half the frosting over it. Allow a few moments for the molten topping to sink into the holes then use the rest to spread a second layer on the cake. Sprinkle *Daim* balls all over to decorate. Don't worry if it looks rather messy – that's half the fun. Serve just as it is or with a dollop of sour cream. If there's any left over (and there seldom is), it can be stored in an airtight container for 2-3 days.

Mustikkapiirakka (Finnish blueberry tart)

This is a brilliant recipe from my friend Eleonoora who, like me, loves Scandinavian wild blueberries (bilberries). If you aren't able to get hold of any, then try this with farmed blueberries, raspberries, blackberries, gooseberries, mixed summer berries, cherries or even lovely ripe plums. If vanilla extract doesn't appeal, try substituting spices like cinnamon or star anise, or maybe some orange or lemon rind, fresh orange juice or orange extract – and a splash of brandy, Grand Marnier or cherry liqueur wouldn't go amiss! Be warned, this is a BIG tart to be shared with family and friends…

SERVES 12-16

cardomon cream bun
   dough (page 137,
   Afternoon Cake)
800g fresh or
   frozen blueberries
100g fructose
   (or 150g caster sugar)
2 tbsp corn flour
1 tbsp vanilla extract
juice of 1 large lemon
1 egg, lightly beaten
   to glaze

Follow the cardamom cream bun dough recipe up to and including the second proving, although obviously you do not divide the mixture in to buns after the first proving, but instead leave it to prove both times as a single large ball of dough.

Mix the berries, fructose, corn flour, vanilla extract and lemon juice in a large bowl. There are then two ways in which you can assemble this tart; you can either follow the traditional method which just uses the edges of the dough itself to hold the berries in place or, if you'd rather, you can use a large rectangular cake tin (at least 30cm x 40cm) to give the tart more structure and make it a bit easier to handle.

Traditional method: Roll out the cardamom bun dough with a rolling pin to form a round base for the pie, approximately 2.5cm thick. Carefully tip the berry mix in the middle of the pie base, leaving the outermost 5cm of dough around the edge free of berries. Using a dough scraper or palette knife, fold the edge of dough in and over so it slightly covers the berries. Brush the edges with beaten egg.

Tin method: Roll the dough in to a rectangle slightly larger than the 30cm x 40cm rectangular cake tin, place the dough in the tin, spread the berry filling over the base, leaving about 1cm or so at the edge. Brush the edges with beaten egg.

Bake on the upper middle shelf of the oven at 200°C/180°C fan/gas mark 6 for 15 minutes, then turn the heat down to 180°C/160°C fan/gas mark 4 and cook for a further 15 minutes. By this time the dough should be golden brown and feel firm to the touch, and the blueberries will be a deep inky black colour.

This is a tart to be shared with friends, so present it in its glorious entirety while still warm, before cutting and dishing out at the table. It doesn't need any embellishment as it's fabulous straight from the oven, but if you fancy it, you could serve it with some crème fraiche or vanilla ice cream. If you don't manage to finish it all on the day of baking, wrap it in foil or pop it in an airtight container and it will keep for a day or two. Otherwise you could freeze it and reheat in the oven to refresh it before serving.

Mama Johansen's plum muffins

My mother bakes these plum muffins for me when I go home to visit. They're my favourite teatime treat and taste best when made with ripe plums in season. They freeze remarkably well and are a wonderful treat reheated in the oven on a cold winter's morning when fresh plums are a distant summer memory. If you can't find unwaxed oranges, just give a regular one a good wash and scrub to remove any wax from the peel.

MAKES 12 MUFFINS

120g butter
250g refined spelt (or plain) flour
170g golden caster sugar
1 tsp baking powder
½ tsp bicarbonate of soda
¼ tsp salt
150ml plain wholemilk or Greek yoghurt
2 medium eggs
1 tsp vanilla extract
12 plums, pitted and cut into eighths
zest of 1 unwaxed orange

Preheat the oven to 190°C/170°C fan/gas mark 5 and line a 12-cup muffin tin with muffin cups or parchment paper, or simply oil the insides of each cup.

Melt the butter (in a bowl over simmering water or in the microwave) and leave it to cool while you sift the flour, sugar, baking powder, bicarbonate of soda and salt into a large bowl, mix thoroughly and then make a well in the middle. Mix the yoghurt, eggs and vanilla extract in a separate bowl, then add the cooled butter and stir well before pouring everything into the dry ingredients. Combine using a large metal spoon, folding just enough times so that the mixture looks even (a friend of mine swears that 12 times should be the maximum – see what you think!) Add the chopped plums and orange zest and stir a few more times to incorporate them.

Using an ice cream scoop or teaspoon, scoop the muffin mixture in to the muffin cups, filling each one about two-thirds full. Bake on the upper-middle shelf of the oven for 15 minutes or until the muffins look golden brown and feel firm to the touch. These keep for a day or two wrapped in foil or in an airtight container, or you can freeze them in foil to keep for 2-3 months.

Chocolate mocha coconut muffins

Coconut and chocolate is a popular pairing in Scandinavia and always reminds me of eating chocolate coconut cake at friends' birthday parties when I was a child. The classic Scandinavian version uses milk chocolate but I prefer the intensity of dark. The combination of dark chocolate and coffee makes these muffins rather more grown-up. They're a doddle to make and the high moisture content from the sour cream and muscovado sugar keeps them fresh for a couple of days if stored in an airtight container. If you don't have any sour cream, use whole-milk yoghurt or half-fat crème fraiche instead.

MAKES 12 MUFFINS

100g dark chocolate
100g butter
3 tbsp cocoa powder
1 shot espresso or 1 tsp instant coffee
  granules dissolved in 1 tbsp hot water
200g refined spelt (or plain) flour
150g light brown muscovado sugar
¼ tsp salt
1 tsp baking powder
½ tsp bicarbonate of soda
2 medium eggs, beaten

100ml sour cream
1 tsp vanilla extract
1-2 tbsp milk or water to thin (if needed)
Glaze
100g butter
100g dark chocolate
1 heaped tbsp cocoa powder
1 tbsp strong coffee
1 tsp vanilla extract
50g icing sugar, sifted
handful desiccated coconut

Preheat the oven to 180°C/160°C fan/gas mark 4 and line a 12-cup muffin tin with muffin cups or parchment paper, or simply oil the insides of each cup.

Put the chocolate, butter, cocoa powder and coffee in a heatproof bowl over a small saucepan containing a couple of centimetres of simmering water. Allow the mixture to melt to a smooth liquid and then take off the heat to cool slightly.

Sift the flour, sugar, salt and raising agents in to a large bowl, stir together and make a well in the middle. Add the beaten eggs, sour cream and vanilla extract, and stir through 3-4 times before stirring in the melted chocolate mix. If the mixture is very dense, add a couple of tablespoons of milk or water to thin it a little, until it has a thick mousse-like consistency.

Use an ice cream scoop or dessert spoon to scoop the mixture in to the muffin cases, filling them about two-thirds full. Bake for 20-25 minutes on the upper-middle shelf of the oven until firm to the touch. Leave to cool on a wire rack while you make the glaze.

Melt the butter, chocolate, cocoa and coffee in a heatproof bowl over simmering water, and then remove from the heat and add the vanilla and icing sugar, stirring well to combine in to a smooth icing. Use to glaze the cooled muffins and sprinkle with desiccated coconut to finish. I heartily recommend that you sit down and devour one or two immediately, accompanied by a sigh of satisfaction and a hot cup of coffee or green tea.

Saffransskorpor
(Swedish saffron and choc chip biscuits)

These cheerful yellow saffron and chocolate chip biscotti-like biscuits are a Swedish tradition and make great gifts. Skorpor (literally 'rusks') keep really well for up to a month in an airtight container, so why not put some in a biscuit tin near the kettle for those moments when you feel like snacking on a little something with your coffee or tea. If you fancy making a nutty version, substitute the same weight of toasted almonds, hazelnuts or walnuts for the chocolate chips.

MAKES 45-50 BISCUITS

100g butter, softened
175g golden caster sugar
1 tsp vanilla extract
1g (or a pinch) saffron strands

3 medium eggs
350g refined spelt (or plain) flour
1 tbsp baking powder
¼ tsp salt
1-2 tbsp milk or water to

loosen the dough (if needed)
100g dark chocolate chips or chopped chocolate
5-6 tbsp natural sugar crystals

Line a baking tray with a sheet of parchment paper.

Use an electric mixer to cream the butter, sugar, vanilla extract and saffron in a large bowl for 3-5 minutes until light and fluffy. Beat the eggs in one at a time, along with a tablespoon of flour each time to stop the mixture from splitting. Mix the remaining flour with the baking powder and salt in a medium bowl and beat this into the butter and egg mixture in two batches (if using plain flour, mix with a metal spoon rather than beating). If the dough is very dry, add a few tablespoons of milk or water to loosen it, being careful not to make the dough too wet. Finally mix in the chocolate chips and divide the dough into four equal-sized lumps.

Roll each quarter in to a log about 25cm long. Place the dough logs on the baking sheet at least 8cm apart and chill in the coolest part of the fridge for 30 minutes to relax the dough.

Preheat the oven to 180°C/160°C fan/gas mark 4 then remove the logs from the fridge and scatter them with sugar crystals down their lengths, before baking them on the middle shelf of the oven for 25 minutes.

Remove the baking tray from the oven and turn the temperature down to 100°C. Allow the logs to cool on the tray for 10-15 minutes before you put them on a chopping board and slice them into 2cm-wide biscotti-style *skorpor*. Put the cut *skorpor* biscuits on the baking sheet and put them back in the oven to bake for a further 50 minutes, turning them the other way up after 25 minutes so that they bake on each side until they completely dry out. If in doubt take one out and let it cool – it should be crispy and crunchy with no moisture in the middle.

Cool on a wire rack and then store in an airtight container or seal in small transparent plastic bags to give as gifts when the occasion calls for it.

Kokosmakroner
(Norwegian coconut macaroons)

These easy-to-make mallowy macaroons are traditionally baked at Christmas time in Norway. I bake them year-round and find that it's worth making several batches at a time as they are always popular. Kokosmakroner *keep for up to 2 weeks in an airtight container, and the coconut keeps them moist so they stay soft for ages. Do make sure to include the salt as it augments all the flavours – I've tried making these without it and they weren't a patch on the real thing. They're utterly more-ish just as they are, but if you're feeling devilish, try dipping them in melted milk or dark chocolate for a decadent treat.*

MAKES 40 LARGE OR 50-60 SMALL MACAROONS

4 egg whites
180g caster sugar
½ tsp vanilla extract
½ tsp salt
250g shredded coconut

Preheat the oven to 170°C/150°C fan/gas mark 3 and line a baking tray with parchment paper or a reusable silicone sheet.

Put the egg whites, sugar, vanilla and salt in a large bowl and beat with an electric whisk or mixer until they hold stiff peaks. Gently fold in the coconut with a metal spoon until it is mixed through, taking care not to knock out too much air from the whisked egg white. Use a dessertspoon to dollop the coconutty meringue mix in little heaps on the baking sheet, leaving 1-2 centimetres between each one.

Bake on the middle shelf of the oven for 10-15 minutes until golden – when they're done, they should feel dry when you touch the tops but still be mallowy inside. Slide the cooked *makroner* carefully off the baking sheet and leave to cool and dry out on a wire rack before eating or storing in an airtight container.

Lemony choux buns

Lemony choux buns are a fabulous, retro alternative to classic afternoon tea cakes. Choux pastry (rather pragmatically called vannbakkels, *or water pastry, in Norwegian) is the only one that my warm bread-baking hands don't completely play havoc with, so I have a particular bias in favour of this light, crisp pastry. My Norwegian grandmother used to bake choux in a large square with a pink sugar glaze, whereas I prefer the individual dainty bun format, as they look so pretty when stacked on a plate. I love the citrus tang of lemon as a contrast to the eggy pastry but you could vary the flavour by using oranges, limes, clementines or passion fruit, or why not try crushed and sieved raspberries, which lend a wonderful natural pink colour to the glaze. Sadly my grandmother never wrote her recipe down, so this one comes from my trusted* Leith's Cookery Bible *and is therefore as foolproof as choux pastry recipes get. If you want to make these in advance, you can freeze the uncooked pastry in dollops on parchment sheets to defrost and bake another day.*

220ml cold water	3 medium eggs, beaten
85g unsalted butter,	Lemony glaze
cubed	200g golden icing sugar
105g refined spelt	zest of 1 lemon
(or plain) flour	(unwaxed or pre-washed)
pinch of salt	4 tbsp lemon juice

Preheat the oven to 200°C/180°C fan/gas mark 6 and line a baking tray with silicone paper. Fold a sheet of parchment or baking paper in half so that it has a crease running down the middle and then open it out again.

Put the water and butter in a medium saucepan over a moderate heat, stirring to make sure that the butter has melted completely before the water reaches the boil.

While the water is heating, sift the flour and salt together on to the parchment paper and repeat twice (this is partly to aerate the flour, and partly baker's superstition!) Once the butter and water are boiling, use the parchment paper to make a funnel and tip the flour and salt in to the boiling liquid. Turn the heat off immediately and stir the mixture for about 20 seconds until it is thick, gloopy and comes away from the sides of the saucepan.

Spread the mixture on a small plate and allow to cool for 10 minutes, then place the cooled dough back in the saucepan off the heat. Add the beaten egg little by little, making sure that each addition is fully mixed in before adding the next, until you have used it all and the mixture reaches a smooth dropping consistency. You don't want choux pastry to be either too runny or too dense: it should drop from the spoon, but reluctantly! Use two teaspoons to place dollops of choux on the baking sheet – a heaped teaspoonful-sized dollop for small choux or pingpong ball-sized for giant choux – leaving 3-5 centimetres between them. Smooth over any rough edges with a spoon dipped in water.

Bake on the top shelf of the oven for 15-20 minutes. It's very important not to open the oven door for at least the first 10 minutes as this could lead to the choux buns collapsing. When they look puffed up and golden, remove them from the oven, pierce the side of each one with a skewer and hollow out any uncooked choux mixture before placing them back in the oven for 5-10 minutes to completely dry out. Allow to cool on a wire rack before glazing.

To make the lemon glaze, sift the icing sugar into a medium bowl and add the lemon zest. Make a well in the middle of the sugar and add the lemon juice, stirring with a wooden spoon until it forms a glaze. Once the choux buns have cooled, dip each one in icing before placing on a plate or wire rack to dry before serving. Choux pastry does not keep well (although un-iced buns can be popped in the oven at 150°C/130°C fan/gas mark 2 for 5-10 minutes to crisp up again if they go a bit soft); however, this is simply a great excuse to eat all these buns on the day of baking.

Fastelavensboller or *semlor*
(Scandinavian cardamom cream buns)

In Scandinavia we mark the arrival of Lent with fastelavensboller (Norway and Denmark) or semlor (Sweden) – yeasty cardamom buns filled with vanilla cream and marzipan. This recipe is adapted from one by Danish chef Trina Hahnemann. The baked but uncut, unfilled buns can be stored for a day or two in an airtight container before filling, or you could freeze them to eat at a later date. You can increase the sugar content by a couple of tablespoons if you like a sweeter bun. If you're using this dough to make the Finnish blueberry tart, follow the recipe up to the end of the second proving.

MAKES 14

25g fresh yeast
375ml lukewarm whole milk
50g butter, melted and slightly cooled
500g refined spelt (or plain) flour
1 tsp ground cardamom
3 tbsp caster sugar
1 tsp salt

1 medium egg beaten (plus additional
    beaten egg to glaze)
Filling
300ml whipping cream
1 tsp vanilla extract
2 tbsp caster sugar
100g marzipan, or more if preferred

Dissolve the yeast in the lukewarm milk in a bowl. Add the melted butter and stir through. Sift the flour, cardamom, sugar and salt together in a large bowl and then stir the milk mixture and one beaten egg in with a large spoon until you get a sticky dough.

Turn the dough on to a floured work surface and knead for 5 minutes until it starts to feel smooth and elastic. You may want to use a dough scraper during the early stages of kneading. Put the kneaded dough back in the mixing bowl, cover with a damp tea towel and put in a warm place to rise. Leave it for about 1-1½ hours until it has doubled in size.

Tip the dough on to a floured work surface and punch once or twice to knock it back. Knead in to a log, then slice into 14 pieces of roughly equal size. Shape these into balls and carefully place them on some parchment paper on a large baking tray. Cover with a damp tea towel and leave in a warm place to prove and double in size again (20-30 minutes).

Preheat the oven to 200°C/180°C fan/gas mark 6 while the buns are proving. Once they have risen, lightly glaze each bun with a little beaten egg and bake on the upper shelf of the oven for 20-25 minutes.

Allow to cool on a wire rack while you lightly whip the cream with the vanilla extract and sugar in a medium bowl. Cut the marzipan in 30-40 thin slices – I use a clean handheld cheese slice or sharp knife. Slice the buns in half and place 2-3 marzipan slices on each bottom half. Spoon or pipe a generous helping of cream on to the marzipan, carefully place the bun 'lid' on top and dust with icing sugar. Serve piled high on a plate, with spiced blueberry juice (page 111, Afternoon Cake) to accompany. Eat with messy enthusiasm!

Dinner

Dinner

Scandinavians believe that taking the time to eat meals together, whether with family or friends, is essential to a good quality of life. My mother insisted on this when I was growing up, and throughout my childhood and teenage years I sat down to eat with my parents every night. This family meal not only gave us all the opportunity to discuss the day we'd had and our plans for tomorrow, but also meant that we could appreciate and enjoy the meal that had been made for us, with all the time and love that involved.

Dinner doesn't have to be anything fancy or complicated; some of my happiest childhood food memories involve tasty soups — fresh crayfish bisque, hearty fish chowder in winter and chilled cucumber soup on the warmest of summer evenings. Then there are the Scandinavian specialties like Norwegian meatballs with mash and red cabbage, creamy anchovy and potato gratin, and of course fish of all kinds, grilled, cured, salted and smoked.

I'm a big fan of the Nordic tradition of *kveldsmat*, or lighter supper dishes, too. If you've scoffed a big Sunday lunch and don't feel like a proper evening meal, then why not round off the day with a simple bowl of cinnamony *rømmegrøt* porridge, or a pile of evening pancakes with fresh berries? If you prefer savoury fare, then a slice or two of Scandi cheese on toast, golden and bubbling straight from the grill, is the tastiest of *kveldsmat* snacks…

Bergensk fiskesuppe (Bergen fish chowder)

Crayfish soup

Chilled cucumber and borage soup

Beetroot and ginger soup

The secret to salting cod

The secret to curing fish

Gravlaks with dill mustard sauce

Speedy citrus-cured halibut

Pickled herring

Baked trout in crème fraiche

Grilled mackerel with kale, potatoes and gooseberries

Mussels with sherry, celeriac and tarragon

Poached egg, mushroom and beetroot salad

Janssons frestelse (Swedish anchovy and potato gratin)

Moose with chanterelles and lingonberry sauce

Roast allspice chicken

Scandilicious macaroni cheese

Norwegian meatballs

Meatball gravy

Mashed swede and potato

Spiced lingonberry red cabbage

Kveldsmat evening pancakes

Wild garlic and *Västerbotten* omelette

Grilled *Jarlsberg* on toast

Rømmegrøt (Norwegian sour cream porridge)

Bergensk fiskesuppe
(Bergen fish chowder)

Growing up in Bergen, a town with rich maritime traditions on the west coast of Norway, this was (and still is) one of my Dad's favourite soups. It's also one of mine as it's so easy to make, wholesome and hearty for cool autumn or winter nights. The mix of seafood gives this dish real depth. Use whatever you have available – razor clams, crayfish, gurnard, hake, John Dory, turbot – as this chowder will taste delicious with any number of fish and shellfish combinations.

SERVES 4

100g cooked shell-on North Sea prawns
1½ litres fish stock
1 bay leaf
handful parsley
12 whole peppercorns
2 carrots, roughly diced
2 celery stalks, roughly diced
1 leek, thinly sliced
100ml dry white wine
50ml brandy
300ml double cream
100g salmon fillet, cubed into 2cm pieces
150g pollack fillet (or haddock or cod), cubed into 2cm pieces
100g scallops (or mussels or clams), without shells
chives to garnish

Shell the prawns and put them in a large saucepan with the fish stock, bay leaf, parsley, peppercorns, carrots, celery and leek and simmer for 10-15 minutes. Pour in the white wine and brandy, simmer for another 5 minutes, then add the double cream and bring back to a simmer. Put the salmon, pollack and scallops in and cook for a further 3-4 minutes before adding the cooked prawns to warm through (they'll probably need less than a minute). Season to taste.

Serve garnished with finely chopped chives, alongside a big dish of steamed potatoes and a pile of buttered crispbread or toast.

Crayfish soup

Few things evoke summer for me as much as crayfish. One year my Dad discovered an abundance in the local fjord – for some reason the locals didn't fish for them. We caught hundreds. That year and for a number of summers after that, we regularly feasted on freshly barbecued crayfish. The Swedes and Finns traditionally hold crayfish parties in August and eat huge quantities of these tasty critters. Any crayfish that don't go to the parties can be used to make this delicious Scandinavian take on lobster bisque.

SERVES 4

1kg shell-on wild crayfish
2 tbsp vegetable oil
100g butter
2 shallots, finely chopped
juice of 1 lemon
50ml brandy
1 litre fish stock
1 bay leaf
1 stalk parsley
2 star anise
200g crème fraiche
1 small pot (c.100g) salmon roe
handful dill, roughly shredded

Peel all the uncooked crayfish or, if you prefer, peel all but 4 to set aside as garnish for the final dish. Peeling them should be straightforward but if you get a couple of tough ones, use nutcrackers or give them a gentle tap with a rolling pin or mallet (or a hammer!) Heat the oil and 20g of the butter in a large saucepan. Fry the crayfish shells for 2 minutes, then add the shallots, lemon juice and brandy and cook for a further 2 minutes. Add the fish stock, bay leaf, parsley and star anise and simmer for 30 minutes to extract flavour and colour from the crayfish shells. Fish out the shells and discard.

Gently poach the peeled crayfish in the broth until they are opaque and cooked through, then remove with a sieve or slotted spoon. Blitz the cooked crayfish in a blender with the remaining 80g of butter (or pound the crayfish with a meat tenderiser or rolling pin to break it up before combining with the butter in a large bowl). The mixture should have the same slightly chunky consistency as dressed crab. Then whisk in to the bisque for added texture and flavour. Season the soup to taste with salt and pepper, and serve in deep bowls garnished with a dollop of crème fraiche, a generous tablespoonful of salmon roe and a pinch of dill fronds.

Chilled cucumber and borage soup

Cold, crisp, cleansing green soup. Perfect for sultry summer nights when you can't face cooking. This can be knocked up in under 15 minutes and tastes so delicious that you'll want to make it again and again. You don't have to throw the cucumber seeds away – you can add them to salads or eat them as they are. Borage, incidentally, is a perfect partner for cucumber on account of its cucumber-like flavour, and it's one of the key ingredients in Pimm's cocktails, so it gives you a marvellous excuse to make a cocktail or two to accompany the soup. Hurrah, I say! If you can't find borage, then use mint, dill, parsley, tarragon, fennel fronds or wood sorrel instead. If you want to embellish a little, why not add some North Sea shrimp, salmon roe or flaked hot smoked trout scattered over the soup just before serving?

SERVES 2

1 large banana shallot, finely chopped
1 tsp oil
1 large cucumber, halved and seeded
300ml vegetable or chicken stock
1 bunch borage, stalks removed
white pepper, freshly ground
1 small pot (250-300ml) sour cream to garnish

Sweat the shallot in the oil in a small frying pan over a low heat for 5 minutes until translucent. Put the cucumber, stock and borage leaves in a blender and blitz until you have a smooth, Kermit-the-Frog green liquid. Stir in a small pinch of pepper and taste to see if it needs more. The stock should be salty enough to season the soup on its own, but do add a pinch of salt if you think it needs it.

Chill for a few hours and then serve in wide bowls with a splodge of sour cream in the middle of the soup. If you're feeling summery and frivolous, garnish with borage flowers or any other edible flowers you may have.

Beetroot and ginger soup

This soup is adapted from an old favourite Leiths' recipe. It manages to be 'virtuous' and healthy, while tasting fantastic. It's great if you're feeling a bit under the weather, or just need a break from too much afternoon cake. I recommend using A Vogel's Herbamare salt if you can get hold of it, otherwise use a pinch of sea salt and mixed herbs.

SERVES 4

1 onion, roughly chopped
1 carrot, roughly chopped
1 celery stick, roughly chopped
2 tbsp oil
2 star anise
½ tsp ground allspice
½ tsp ground juniper berries
½ tsp nutmeg, finely grated
½ tsp ground ginger
5cm piece of ginger, peeled and grated
450g cooked beetroot (not pickled), roughly chopped
800ml hot vegetable stock
1-2 tbsp lemon, basil, bay and juniper vinegar (or cider vinegar)
1-2 tbsp aquavit (or gin or vodka)
pinch of A Vogel's Herbamare salt
pinch of pepper
4 tbsp sour cream (or crème fraiche or Greek yoghurt) (optional)
chives, chopped (optional)

Start by sweating the onion, carrot and celery in the oil in a large saucepan over a low heat until soft. Stir in the dried spices and half the fresh ginger and continue to stir while cooking for a minute or so. Add the beetroot, stock, vinegar, aquavit, salt and pepper, bring to a simmer and cook over a low-medium heat for 15-20 minutes. Blitz the soup with a handheld blender or in a heatproof glass blender until smooth. If you're using an upright liquidiser, do make sure that the lid is securely on – I keep a tea towel pressed firmly on top just to make sure that the soup doesn't erupt and force the lid off when I start blending. Return the soup to the pan and check the seasoning, adding more salt, pepper and fresh ginger to taste.

Heat through and serve in bowls, either just as it is or topped with a dollop of sour cream and a sprinkle of chopped chives.

The secret to salting cod

Salt cod is enjoyed throughout Europe from northern Scandinavia to southern Spain, Italy and Portugal. There are three main secrets to salting cod – you need (1) super-fresh fish, (2) storage in cold windy conditions and (3) really good sea salt. So, unless you happen to have access to a shed in the outer Hebrides, you're unlikely to be salting and drying your own on a regular basis. The short-cut method is simply to soak one large fillet of fresh cod overnight in 800ml of water and 240g of sea salt.

In Bergen my grandmother would often get lettsaltet torsk *(lightly salted cod) from the fishmongers. She would rinse it under cold running water for 30 minutes (or up to an hour if it was heavily salted) and then poach it in a shallow pan of barely simmering water for 5-8 minutes, depending on the thickness of the fillets (if you're feeling decadent, try poaching it in butter instead. It gives it a wonderful mellow flavour).*

Traditionally, salt cod is partnered with leek butter in Norway – it's not a low calorie option, but it is utterly delicious. Sweat a large leek in a little butter and oil, season with A Vogel's Herbamare salt (or sea salt) once the leek is soft and translucent and then melt a 250g pack of butter in the pan with the leeks. Serve the hot poached cod covered with leek butter and accompanied by steamed new potatoes, carrots and peas for a truly retro meal.

The secret to curing fish

Be it gravlaks *(known in Swedish as* gravadlax*), smoked fish eggs, pickled herring or the highly fragrant* surströmming *(Swedish fermented herring), curing and preserving fish has been a mainstay of Scandinavian life for centuries. The process improves the flavour, texture and longevity of the fish, as well as giving you a real taste of Scandinavia!*

Gravlaks with dill mustard sauce

The key to this classic Scandinavian dish is an exceptionally fresh fillet of salmon.
If in doubt, freeze the fillet for 24 hours to kill any bacteria, then defrost it.
This traditional gravlaks cure is slightly more sweet than salty, but you can always use
equal quantities of sugar and salt if you prefer. If you're feeling adventurous, try adding
beetroot, alcohol (aquavit, gin or vodka) or juniper berries to the cure.

MAKES ENOUGH FOR 12-14 STARTERS OR 6-8 *SMÖRGÅSBORD* BRUNCHES

1½ kg salmon fillet, cut in half

1 tbsp white peppercorns

2 tbsp coriander seeds

100g granulated sugar

75g sea salt

3 x 15g pack dill, chopped (for the cure)

1 x 15g pack dill, chopped (to serve)

Dill mustard sauce

1 x 15g pack dill

3 tbsp vegetable oil

3 tbsp white wine or cider vinegar

3 tbsp demerara sugar

3 tbsp mustard

½ tsp salt

Dry the salmon, check for pinbones and then place both fillet pieces side by side, skin down. Crush the white pepper and coriander with a pestle and mortar and then mix in a small bowl with the sugar and salt. Spread the dill over the skinless side of the fillet halves, then spread the spiced sugar and salt in a layer on top. Sandwich both fillets together so that the dill spice mixture is in the middle and the skin is outermost. Cover any exposed surface of salmon with any dill and spice mixture that tumbles out. Wrap very tightly in two layers of clingfilm and place in a small roasting tin to catch the brine that escapes the fish as it cures. Refrigerate for a minimum of 24 hours and up to 48 hours.

The dill mustard sauce is very easy to make. You just whizz up all the ingredients in a blender. You can then either use it straight away or keep it in an airtight glass jar in the fridge for a week or so.

When the gravlaks has had time to cure, simply take it out of the fridge, remove the clingfilm, wipe the fillet halves clean of the herby spiced salt with a paper towel, pat dry and put on a board, skin down. Put a layer of chopped dill on the skinless side of each fillet and press down as much as you can without squashing the fish. Slice on the diagonal from the tail towards the middle of the fillet and serve with hot new potatoes, rye or sourdough bread and dill mustard sauce.

Speedy citrus-cured halibut

Grilled halibut steaks were something of a favourite with my parents when we lived in Oslo and it was one of the first cooked white fish that I really learnt to love. Despite this, I've decided to forgo a grilled halibut recipe in favour of a cured one! I picked up the idea for juniper salt at Copenhagen's famous Noma restaurant. It is very versatile and works brilliantly with chicken, lamb, fish, salads and vegetables.

SERVES 6 AS A STARTER

zest and juice of 3 large unwaxed (or well-scrubbed) lemons
2-3 tbsp lemon, basil, bay and juniper vinegar (or cider vinegar)
1 tbsp gin or aquavit
1 tsp fructose (or 1½ tsp caster sugar)
450g halibut, skinned and boned
2 shallots
1 fennel bulb (plus fronds to garnish)
6 radishes
1 tsp crushed juniper berries to garnish

Zest the lemons with a microplane or fine zester on to a small plate (to be used later) before juicing them. Mix the lemon juice, vinegar, alcohol, fructose and a pinch of salt and white pepper in a medium bowl. Taste it – it should be sour but aromatic. Cut the halibut in to 0.5cm thick slices (slicing horizontally along the fillet, as you would with *gravlaks*) – the thinner you can slice it, the more delicate the texture of the cured fish.

Put the halibut slices in the marinade and mix with your hands to make sure that they are fully coated. If you want to tenderise the shallot, fennel and radish slightly, then slice them very finely and add to the mix. If not, leave them unsliced until you're ready to serve. Cover the marinade bowl and refrigerate for 1 hour, taking it out once or twice while the fish is curing to give everything a good stir, to make sure that the marinade is evenly distributed.

When you're ready to serve, share the slices between 6 plates and sprinkle the lemon zest over them for an extra spritz of citrus, followed by a sprinkle of chopped fennel fronds. Mix the crushed juniper berries with three teaspoons of sea salt and place a small pot of this herby salt by each plate, so everyone can help themselves.

Pickled herring

Historically, herring formed a crucial part of the diet throughout northern Europe. I love the variety of cured herring you can find across Scandinavia, but my favourite is still sursild, *herring pickled in a sweet-sour brine and lots of spices. This nutritious and delicious dish is great as part of a* smörgåsbord *and plays a central role in Nordic Christmas entertaining. Simply serve with cooked potatoes, rye bread, sour cream and herbs of your choice. I find that it's worth pickling large quantities of herring in spring and summer when they're plentiful, as they last for a good few months in the fridge. I use a 750ml-1l capacity glass jar for this recipe, but you could use 3 or 4 smaller 227g jars instead.*

SERVES 6

6 salted herrings
300ml white wine or
  cider vinegar
250ml water
50ml aquavit (or water)
175g caster sugar
1 tsp salt
10 allspice berries

1 tbsp peppercorns
1 tbsp mustard seeds
1 tsp coriander seeds
5 cloves
4 dried juniper berries
1 fresh bay leaf
1 large sprig dill, chopped
2 shallots, thinly sliced

Soak the salted herring for 2 hours or as recommended by your fishmonger. Simmer the vinegar, water, aquavit, sugar, salt and all the spices in a medium saucepan. Once the caster sugar has completely dissolved, turn the heat down to a gentle simmer for 10 minutes. Set aside and leave to cool.

Preheat the oven to 100°C while you wash a large (750ml-1l capacity) glass jar, then pop it in the oven for 10 minutes to dry and sterilise it. Put half the dill fronds and one-third of the sliced shallots in the bottom.

Rinse the herring, dry with kitchen paper, remove any skin and pinbones and then cut into 2cm pieces. Put half the chopped herring in the jar, followed by half the remaining shallot and dill and pour in half the spice-filled brine mixture (if you want a clearer brine, feel free to strain the spices out first). Repeat with the remaining herring and other ingredients and top with the brine, ensuring that it completely covers the herring.

Seal the glass jar and store in the fridge for at least 5 days before eating. The longer you keep the pickled herring in the brine, the more tender it becomes and the more intense the sweet-sour flavour. This will keep refrigerated for a couple of months.

Baked trout in crème fraiche

This simple baked trout recipe always reminds me of late summer, when Dad would go up in to the mountains in western Norway and fish for trout. The haul of fresh fish arriving back at the farm was always fun to peer at. I think this is one of the best ways to eat fresh trout. I recommend using A Vogel's Herbamare salt if you can get hold of it, otherwise use a pinch of sea salt and mixed herbs.

SERVES 2-4

2 tbsp clarified butter (or vegetable oil)
2 medium trout, descaled and filleted
juice of ½ lemon

2 tbsp brandy
300ml crème fraiche
pinch of A Vogel's Herbamare salt

Preheat the oven to 200°C/180°C fan/gas mark 6.

Heat the clarified butter in a large ovenproof skillet or frying pan until very hot. Season and fry the fish fillets skin-side down for 1-2 minutes to crisp the skin and partially cook the trout. Flip the trout over so the skin side faces upwards. Add the lemon juice and brandy and cook for a further minute, then add the crème fraiche and salt.

Remove from the heat and transfer to the upper-middle shelf of the oven. Bake for 10-15 minutes or until the sauce starts to look golden and is bubbling vigorously. Serve while hot either on its own, or with a green salad and perhaps some new potatoes.

Grilled mackerel with kale, potatoes and gooseberries

Make sure you buy mackerel that's really fresh: it should only have a faint smell of the sea. The flavours in this dish balance brilliantly – the sharpness of the traditional gooseberry compote cuts through the oiliness of the fish, and the sautéed green kale is fresh, tender and tasty.

SERVES 4

250g new potatoes
vegetable oil for roasting
250g gooseberries
3 tbsp fructose
 (or 4½ tbsp caster sugar)
½ cup water
2 shallots

50g butter
4 large mackerel fillets (or small
 whole mackerel)
vegetable oil for grilling the fish
300g curly kale, washed, stalks
 removed, roughly chopped
1 lemon, quartered, to garnish

Preheat oven to 180°C/160°C fan/gas mark 4.

Parboil the new potatoes in salted water in a medium pan for 5 minutes, drain and allow the potatoes to dry for a couple of minutes in the pan over a low heat so all excess water evaporates. Remove from the pan and halve the new potatoes. Drizzle oil in the bottom of a large roasting tin and sprinkle salt and pepper. Place the new potatoes cut-side down in the tin and drizzle again with oil, sprinkling salt and pepper on top. Roast the potatoes for 30 minutes, then flip them over and roast for another 30 minutes.

In the meantime, bring the gooseberries, fructose and water to the boil in a medium saucepan over a medium-high heat. Once boiling, reduce the heat and simmer the gooseberries for 5-8 minutes until they're broken down and soft.

Finely chop the shallots and sauté gently in the butter for 10 minutes over a low heat. They should be translucent and soft. Set to one side until you are ready to cook the kale.

Preheat the grill to high. Check that the potatoes are fully roasted before grilling the fish as the mackerel will cook in 3-4 minutes. Make three parallel slashes in the skin of each fillet and then oil both sides of the mackerel before seasoning with salt and pepper. Grill the fillets for 1 minute with the exposed flesh upwards, then turn them to grill for 2-3 minutes skin side uppermost, until the skin starts to look golden and crispy. It will bubble and spit but be brave, that's normal when grilling oily fish!

Once you have turned the mackerel over to grill the skin side, put the shallots back on a low-medium heat and add the kale to cook for 2 minutes or so, until wilted.

Put the new potatoes, kale, shallots and gooseberry compote on warmed plates, top with the grilled mackerel and serve immediately with a quarter lemon on each plate to garnish.

Mussels with sherry, celeriac and tarragon

Manzanilla sherry, with its slight salty tang, makes a great partner for seafood. I serve these mussels with chilled manzanilla to drink instead of the usual white wine. The inclusion of celeriac was an idea I picked up in Copenhagen's amazing Fiskebaren *restaurant, but you can omit the celeriac and tarragon and eat the mussels as they are or sprinkled with chopped parsley.*

SERVES 4

2kg mussels
1 head celeriac, peeled and chopped
  into 1cm cubes
1 medium onion, finely chopped
4 shallots, finely chopped
1 tbsp vegetable oil
25g butter (plus 25g cold butter
  for the sauce)
1 sprig tarragon, chopped
  (plus more to garnish)
200ml fish stock
150ml manzanilla sherry
pinch of white pepper
crème fraiche (optional)
zest and juice of ½ lemon

Scrub the mussels under cold water. Pull out the 'beards' (the rough threads coming out of the shell) and throw these away. Tap each mussel gently to check whether it's still alive – the mussel should close upon tapping, so throw out any that remain open. Put the clean drained mussels in a covered bowl or container in the fridge.

Bring a saucepan of salted water to the boil, add the diced celeriac and boil for 2 minutes or until just al dente. Then drain the cooked celeriac in a colander and run cold water over it to stop it cooking further. Leave in the colander while you cook the mussels.

Sauté the chopped onion and shallot in the oil and butter in a large saucepan over a low heat. Allow to sweat for 5-8 minutes or until they look translucent and soft. Add the sprig of tarragon, stock and sherry and simmer for 5 minutes to cook off the alcohol. Add a pinch of white pepper and the crème fraiche (if using), turn up the heat, pour in the mussels and cover with a lid. Steam for 5 minutes or until the mussels have popped wide open. It's worth shaking the pan once or twice to distribute the ingredients.

Use a slotted spoon to remove the mussels from the pan, throwing out any that haven't opened. Keep them in a large pre-warmed bowl or dish and cover (pop them in the oven at 100°C while you finish the sauce, if you want to keep them piping hot). Simmer the sauce until it has reduced by one-third and thickened slightly. Remove the sprig of tarragon and whisk in the cold butter to gloss the sauce and thicken it slightly. Add the celeriac to the sauce and swirl around over a low heat for 1 minute to warm through, then pour over the mussels.

Finish by grating the lemon zest over the steaming bowl and sprinkling with a little lemon juice and extra chopped tarragon. Then stir with a large spoon and put the bowl in the middle of the table for everyone to tuck in and share, with plenty of white bread to soak up the juices.

Poached egg, mushroom and beetroot salad

Foraging for edible wild mushrooms is definitely one of autumn's great pleasures for me. This dish is fresh and bursting with flavour. Great as a tasty lunch for two or a dinnertime starter for four. If you don't have any beetroot leaves, use a selection of other salad leaves instead.

SERVES 2-4

200g beetroot leaves
1 tsp grainy mustard
2 tbsp white wine vinegar
3-4 tbsp walnut oil
150g cooked beetroot, cut into quarters
4 large eggs
400g wild mushrooms (whole or chopped)
1 tbsp vegetable oil
2 tbsp butter
small handful chopped tarragon
toasted walnuts to garnish

Wash the beetroot leaves and set aside to dry. Mix the mustard and vinegar in a bowl and whisk in the walnut oil to create an emulsion. Season with salt and black pepper to taste. Tear the leaves, toss in the dressing and divide between the plates. Scatter the beetroot over the dressed salad.

Bring a couple of centimetres of water to boil in a medium saucepan and then turn the heat right down so that you can only just see a hint of bubbles. Crack each egg into a small bowl or espresso cup, lower to the just-boiling water and then gently drop the egg in. Set your timer for one minute, and once that minute is up, remove the pan from the heat. Re-set your timer to 10 minutes and leave the eggs to cook in the hot water – when the timer goes, you should have perfectly poached eggs.

Once the eggs have been poaching off the heat for a few minutes, fry the mushrooms for 5 minutes in the oil and butter. Add freshly ground black pepper and the chopped tarragon.

By the time you've finished frying the mushrooms, the eggs should be cooked. Remove them from the water with a slotted spoon and drain by holding the spoon on some kitchen towel for a few seconds. Put one egg or two eggs on each salad (depending on whether this is lunch or a starter), divide the fried mushrooms between the plates, scattering them over the salad, and then top with toasted walnuts before serving.

Janssons frestelse
(Swedish anchovy and potato gratin)

Substantial enough to be a meal in itself, Janssons frestelse *(Jansson's temptation) also works well as a side dish with roast lamb or pork, game birds or sautéed white fish. The secret to this dish lies in using the right anchovies. Look for Swedish* ansjos *(technically sprats, but hey, the Swedes call them anchovies) which are pickled in a sweetly savoury, spicy brine and have a milder, more delicate flavour than Italian or Spanish anchovies. The Swedish brand Abba are my favourites, and not just because of the name. I like to use waxy potatoes like Desiree for this dish, but if you prefer a floury potato then I'd use King Edwards or Maris Piper. Krisprolls are toasted Swedish rolls which are used like crispbread – if you can't lay your hands on them, use melba toast instead. You will need a 2 litre shallow Pyrex dish or other ovenproof pan for this recipe, and a mandoline slicer makes life a little easier for slicing the potatoes.*

SERVES 6-8

2 large onions, finely chopped
2 tbsp vegetable oil
1 tin Abba anchovies
4 large potatoes
200ml crème fraiche
170ml double cream
75g white Krisprolls (or melba toast), crushed
25g butter to top

Preheat the oven to 190°C/170°C fan/gas mark 5. Butter the ovenproof dish and set aside.

Sweat the chopped onion in oil in a medium frying pan over a low heat for 5-8 minutes until soft and translucent. Chop the anchovies in half and cut the potatoes in 5mm-thick slices (using a mandoline if you have one). Lay one-third of the potato slices to cover the base of the baking dish and scatter half the anchovies and a quarter of the onion on top. Cover with half the remaining potato slices and then scatter with the rest of the anchovies and another quarter of the onion. Top with a final layer of potato slices.

Tip the remaining half of cooked onion in to a small saucepan, add the crème fraiche, double cream and a good pinch of salt and white pepper and then heat gently until it starts to simmer.

Pour the warm cream mixture over the potatoes and sprinkle with the crushed Krisproll to cover. Dot this crunchy crust with the butter and season with a little salt before placing in the oven to cook for 45-50 minutes, after which time it should look golden brown and crispy on top. Serve while piping hot.

Moose with chanterelles and lingonberry sauce

Moose is a dark gamey meat rather like venison or reindeer. Mild in flavour and low in fat, it makes a great alternative to beef, if you can get hold of it. We once brought half a suitcaseful of Norwegian moose fillet over to England for an eccentric aunt who insisted on having moose for Christmas Eve dinner – it was delicious if rather untraditional! In this dish, the buttered chanterelles go very nicely with the moose... and it wouldn't feel properly Scandinavian if there wasn't a liberal helping of lingonberry sauce too. If you can't find any chanterelles, you can use other wild varieties or Portobello mushrooms instead.

SERVES 4

140g butter (plus 1 tbsp for the sauce)
2 tbsp vegetable oil
800g moose (or venison) fillet
100ml port or Madeira
100g chanterelles, cleaned
1 jar lingonberry sauce

Heat 40g of butter and the oil in a large sauté pan until sizzling and then sear the moose fillet, ensuring that you brown the entire fillet (a pair of tongs is useful for this). Moose fillet is traditionally served rare, so once you've seared the outside, remove it from the pan (which will be used for the sauce) and rest the fillet on a plate covered with foil.

Pour the port or Madeira in the sauté pan and continue to heat, bringing to the boil to cook off the alcohol and to reduce it to a third of its original volume, so you have a sticky glaze. Sieve a spoonful or two of lingonberry sauce, and add a tablespoon of the sieved sauce to the glaze. Season the glaze to taste and finish with a generous tablespoonful of butter to gloss. Keep this warm over a low heat while you prepare the mushrooms.

Melt the remaining tablespoon of butter in a small sauté pan over a medium heat, add the chanterelles and cook for 5 minutes. Season to taste.

Slice the rested moose fillet on the diagonal, divide among the plates and serve immediately with the buttered chanterelles, steamed seasonal greens of your choice, a drizzled spoonful or two of the glaze and lingonberry sauce on the side.

Roast allspice chicken

This is a slight variation on the brilliant chef and food writer Simon Hopkinson's famous roast chicken recipe, using allspice and a pinch of coriander seed instead of thyme and garlic. The allspice adds a subtle alluring aroma that's simultaneously familiar and exotic.

SERVES 4-6

2kg free range chicken
2 tsp allspice berries, freshly ground
1 tsp coriander seed, freshly ground
125g butter, softened
1 lemon, halved

Preheat the oven to 220°C/200°C fan/gas mark 7.

Rinse the chicken and pat dry with kitchen paper. Sieve the ground allspice and coriander seed into the butter and mix well to combine. Don't throw away any coarse bits or strands of spice left in the sieve, as they can be put in the cavity of the chicken later. Season the butter with salt and pepper, then – this is the messy fun part – using your hands, rub the butter all over the chicken. The more vigorous the 'massage', the more even the distribution of butter!

Season the cavity with salt, pepper and any remaining spice bits from the sieve, then stuff half a lemon inside. Sprinkle a pinch of salt over the chicken skin and place along with the other half lemon in a roasting tin.

Roast the chicken for 20 minutes at 220°C/200°C fan/gas mark 7, then turn the heat down to 190°C/170°C fan/gas mark 5. Continue to roast for an hour at this temperature, basting the chicken every 30 minutes or so, until cooked. Use a sharp knife and slice into the drumstick – if the chicken juices run clear, it is done. If the juices still have some blood in them, roast for another five minutes and then check again, repeating until cooked through.

Remove the cooked chicken from the oven and leave to rest on a wooden carving board for a good 15-20 minutes to ensure that the meat remains juicy. Then carve and serve with the allspice butter and lemon sauce gathered from the bottom of the pan.

ALLSPICE CHICKEN STOCK

You can use the allspice chicken carcass (stripped of any leftover meat but with some of the skin and fat left for flavour) to make excellent stock. Place in a large saucepan and cover with cold water for a pure chicken stock, or add chopped carrot, celery and onion (one of each is enough), a bay leaf, a thyme sprig and some allspice berries for a delicious aromatic broth. Then simply simmer uncovered for an hour or two over a lowish heat, skimming any foam from the surface and making sure that the stock doesn't boil or this will create a murky broth. Perfect for soups or just to sip on its own.

Scandilicious macaroni cheese

On a cold winter's night there are few things more delicious than the combination of pasta and hot, oozing cheese. Done properly, mac 'n' cheese is cold climate comfort food of the highest order. The trick is to make it really, really cheesy. This recipe is an adaptation of one I entered in an Ultimate Macaroni Cheese Challenge where it won the prize for 'best use of artisan cheese'… with a prize of more artisan cheese! If you can't get hold of some of these cheeses you could try substituting: a good quality Gouda-type cheese for Svecia; *Parmesan for* Västerbotten; *and Stilton, Gorgonzola or Roquefort for the Danish Blue.*

SERVES 4

250g macaroni
350g crème fraiche
150ml double cream
100g Caerphilly, finely grated
½ clove garlic
100g Danish Blue, crumbled
100g *Västerbotten*, coarsely grated
75g *Svecia*, coarsely grated
50g *Jarlsberg*, shaved or thinly sliced
Worcestershire sauce (optional)

Preheat the oven to 190°C/170°C fan/gas mark 5.

Cook the macaroni in salted water in a small saucepan until al dente – 5 minutes should do it. Drain in a colander and run cold water over the pasta to stop it cooking any further.

Heat the crème fraiche and double cream in a small saucepan until it starts to boil. Take off the heat when it starts to really bubble and stir in the Caerphilly. Season to taste – pasta on its own is pretty bland, so you'll need some salt and pepper in the sauce to give the whole dish oomph!

Rub the halved garlic clove around the inside of a 20cm x 30cm Pyrex or other ovenproof dish – or a 30cm x 40cm one, if you want a bigger surface area for crispy cheese! Tip the pasta in to the cheesy sauce and mix well. Pour in to the roasting dish and sprinkle with the crumbled Danish Blue. Top with the *Västerbotten*, *Svecia* and *Jarlsberg*, then bake uncovered in the oven for 20-25 minutes.

Drizzle the top with Worcestershire sauce for a Welsh Rarebit effect if you fancy it, or simply leave plain. Then blast the dish under a hot grill for a few minutes before serving for a slightly caramelised, crispy topping. Serve, hot and decadently delicious, accompanied by a fresh green salad.

Norwegian meatballs

Although I maintain that Scandinavia has much more to offer than the humble herring and mighty meatball, I secretly crave both these dishes. Who doesn't love meatballs? My American grandfather famously ate 40 of them at my parents' wedding in Norway. While I don't recommend eating quite that many at once, they're great as a main course, as a midnight snack or as leftovers the next day on buttered toast with – whisper it – dollops of tomato ketchup. They always remind me of the Muppet Show's Swedish Chef who starts playing meatball tennis, waving his cooking utensils and shouting 'hurdy gurdy'. Obviously you won't catch me playing meatball tennis, although I might say 'hurdy gurdy' when feeling particularly Scandinavian...

If you can't find lamb or veal mince, substitute beef or pork mince. I like to serve this with mashed swede and potato and spiced lingonberry cabbage, garnished with fresh dill or parsley. If you are making the cabbage, start with this first, as it takes a while to cook down and for the spices to infuse, and if anything the flavours improve if you leave it overnight and simply reheat it the next day.

SERVES 6-8

1 tbsp vegetable oil
1 onion, peeled and finely chopped
1 tbsp ground allspice
1 level tsp ground nutmeg
½ level tsp ground ginger
225ml whole milk, mixed with
  1 tbsp yoghurt
3 slices (c. 110g) stale white bread,
  preferably sourdough
500g veal mince
500g lamb mince
1 large egg yolk
1½ level tsp salt
¼ level tsp black pepper

Preheat the grill to medium-high (unless you are making these in advance). Heat the oil in a pan and cook the onion over a low heat for 8-10 minutes until soft. As the onion goes translucent, add the spices and fry for a minute, then set aside to cool.

In a shallow bowl, pour the yoghurt-milk mixture over the bread, making sure it's all moistened, and leave until the liquid has been absorbed. In a larger bowl, combine the mince, cooked onion, egg yolk and seasoning. Add the milk-soaked bread, then using your hands, mix everything together. Fry a spoonful of the mixture in a little butter and oil and, once cooked, taste it to check that you are happy with the seasoning. Then, taking a teaspoonful of mixture at a time, lightly roll between your palms to form meatballs. Grill straight away or, if you're making these in advance, set aside on a sheet covered with cling-film and keep refrigerated until you're ready. Grill the meatballs for 10-15 minutes until golden brown, turning them once halfway through.

Meatball gravy

Scandinavians traditionally use brown goat's cheese in their stews and gravies. If you can't find it or don't fancy it, you could add an extra dollop of crème fraiche and a teaspoon each of Marmite and brown sugar instead. The grated cacao adds depth of flavour, but if you can't find 100% cacao, try using 70% cocoa chocolate instead.

1 litre good veal or beef stock
100ml brandy
300ml crème fraiche
100g *ekte geitost* (Norwegian brown goat's cheese), grated
2 tbsp grated cacao

Bring the stock to the boil, simmer until reduced by half and then add the brandy. Simmer for a further minute or so until you can't smell any alcohol, then add the crème fraiche, brown cheese and cacao. Season to taste. Add the grilled meatballs to this sauce and simmer for 20 minutes.

Mashed swede and potato

1 large swede, peeled and chopped into large chunks
750g mashing potatoes, peeled and chopped into large chunks
200ml double cream
100g butter

Put the swede and potatoes in cold salted water in two separate saucepans, and boil until soft (10-15 minutes). Drain really thoroughly, then add the swede to the potatoes. Rinse out the swede pan and put the cream in it. Bring to the boil and simmer until reduced by half. Melt the butter into the cream, then gradually add to the swede and potatoes, mashing as you go. Season to taste with salt and pepper.

Spiced lingonberry red cabbage

If you can't find lingonberry jam, use blackcurrant jam, redcurrant jelly or cranberry sauce instead.

2 tbsp butter
1 onion, peeled and sliced
1 apple, peeled and sliced
½ red cabbage, cored and sliced in thin strips
30ml cider vinegar or white wine vinegar
1 generous glass red wine, plus more to taste
5 tbsp lingonberry jam
2 tbsp dark brown sugar
1 cinnamon stick
½ tsp nutmeg
5 whole cloves

Melt the butter in a large saucepan and then add the onion, apple, red cabbage, vinegar, wine and a pinch of salt. Cover and cook for 1 hour, making sure to stir occasionally so that it doesn't burn at the bottom, and adding a little water if it gets dry. When the cabbage is tender, add the lingonberry jam, sugar and spices. Cook for a further 30 minutes and taste for seasoning. A splash of red wine added to the red cabbage before serving wouldn't go amiss.

Kveldsmat evening pancakes

In Scandinavia you'll often come across light supper dishes as an alternative to a full evening meal, a tradition stemming from the days when main meals were eaten at midday or in the late afternoon. My grandparents frequently just had open sandwiches or a bowl of grøt *(porridge). Kveldsmat or 'evening food' is perfect for those days when you don't feel like cooking up a storm at the end of the day, but still fancy a satisfying bite before bedtime.*

In Norway, pancakes are a popular kveldsmat *choice. These are rather different from brunch pancakes (page 51, Brunch) – evening pancakes have a higher proportion of egg and are traditionally eaten with blueberries (bilberries), lingonberries, fruit compotes or just a sprinkle of sugar. In Sweden and Finland, these pancakes are traditionally eaten on a Thursday evening after a steaming bowl of pea and ham soup.*

SERVES 4

3 medium eggs
1 tbsp plain bio yoghurt
500ml whole milk
250g refined spelt (or plain) flour
100g butter, melted
1 tbsp golden caster sugar
½ tsp salt

Beat the eggs and yoghurt with half the milk in a large bowl using a whisk or electric beater. Add the flour and whisk again until the mixture looks smooth and there are no lumps of flour remaining. Add the rest of the milk along with the melted butter, sugar and salt and beat again until the mixture is evenly combined. Cover and pop the bowl in the fridge for 30 minutes while you set the table, make yourself a cup of tea and decide what to put on your pancakes.

Preheat the oven to 100°C and have a plate ready on which to stack the pancakes.

Put a skillet or large non-stick frying pan over a medium-high heat and once it has had a chance to heat up, test with a tablespoon of batter to see whether the pan is hot enough – the batter should bubble up as soon as it hits the surface of the pan. Taste this mini pancake for seasoning and add more salt or sugar to the batter accordingly.

Use a small ladle or a tea cup to pour enough batter for one pancake into the skillet and swirl it around quickly to spread the batter out. Cook for 2 minutes or until the edges of the pancake start to go brown, then flip with a spatula to cook the other side. Another 1-2 minutes on this side should do the trick. Put the finished pancake on the plate and keep warm in the oven. Repeat until all the batter is used up.

Serve the pancakes on four plates or simply put the plated stack, warm from the oven, in the middle of the table and let everyone help themselves.

Wild garlic and *Västerbotten* omelette

Pungent wild garlic, also known as ramsons, is abundant in late spring and early summer, and makes a brilliant ingredient for suppertime omelettes. Just make sure that whoever you kiss goodnight has some as well. You can omit the crème fraiche if you want to make a less creamy omelette.

SERVES 2

4 medium eggs
2 tbsp crème fraiche
2 tbsp vegetable oil
1 banana shallot, finely chopped
4 leaves of wild garlic, chopped
50g *Västerbotten* cheese, grated

Preheat the oven to the lowest setting and put your serving plate in to keep it warm.

Crack the eggs in to a bowl, add the crème fraiche and beat with a whisk or fork until evenly combined.

Heat the oil in a large frying pan over a medium heat, sweat the shallot for 2-3 minutes until soft, then add the wild garlic leaves. Cook for a further minute or so until the leaves wilt, then add the whisked eggs. Tilt the the pan so you get an even distribution of the egg mixture.

Cook until the edge of the omelette is just starting to set but the centre is still soft. Add the grated cheese and a pinch of salt and pepper and then fold the omelette over and cook for a further minute. Serve on the warmed plate while still hot and gooey on the inside. If you want to save on washing up, you can do as my other half and I do and both eat from the same plate. Alternatively slice the omelette in half before serving on two smaller warmed plates. Eat with a green salad and some fresh sourdough or oatmeal bread (page 76, Lunch).

Grilled *Jarlsberg* on toast

Scandi cheese on toast is my fallback dish for those days (usually Sundays) when I just want to make a simple supper with whatever is in the house. Being a cheese fiend I always have some in the fridge and there's invariably half a loaf in the breadbin, so then it's just a matter of pepping things up with some savoury spreads, heaping on the Jarlsberg, *grilling the toast and eating while hot, hot, hot.*

SERVES 2

4 slices bread, preferably sourdough
1 tsp Marmite
2 tsp Savora (or other) mustard
2 tsp chutney

Jarlsberg cheese, sliced
fennel seeds
cayenne pepper

Start by lightly toasting the bread, then spread with the Marmite, mustard and chutney and top with as many slices of *Jarlsberg* as you like. Scatter a few fennel seeds over the cheese and dust with a little cayenne pepper.

Grill for 2-3 minutes on a medium-high setting, keeping an eye on the cheese as it starts to cook, as it can turn from molten cheesy toast to burnt charcoal in no time! Remove from the grill when the cheese is bubbling and has turned golden brown. Serve and eat as soon as decently possible.

Rømmegrøt
(Norwegian sour cream porridge)

Rømmegrøt evokes some of my favourite childhood food memories. Its soothing, delicious sour cream taste is the most comforting thing I can think of, whether eaten on a cool midsummer's evening or a frosty Christmas Eve. This is my grandmother's recipe and makes (in my opinion) quite simply the best rømmegrøt *in the world. I've included her strict instructions to any* rømmegrøt *cook, and the only change I have made has been to suggest using crème fraiche to make up for the fact that Norwegian sour cream tends to have a higher fat content than that found elsewhere.* Rømmegrøt *freezes well so don't worry if you don't have 8 or 10 people to feed this to – you can just serve as much as you need now and freeze the rest. Then when you next fancy some, simply defrost and reheat with extra milk or water.*

SERVES 8-10

1 litre 35+% fat content sour cream (or crème fraiche)
250g semolina
125g refined spelt (or plain) flour
1½ litres whole milk
1-2 tsp salt, plus more to taste
1-2 tbsp golden caster sugar, plus more to taste
cinnamon to taste

Put the sour cream in a large saucepan and bring to an explosive boil (my grandmother's description!), then simmer over a medium heat for about 20 minutes. Stir frequently to ensure that the cream doesn't catch at the bottom of the pan – if necessary, turn the heat down a fraction. After 20 minutes, turn the heat right down to the lowest possible setting.

Mix the semolina and flour together in a medium bowl, then sift in to the warm cream. Whisk vigorously with a large wooden spoon or whisk to get rid of any lumps. Remove from the heat and cover with a lid. After about 20-30 minutes the fat should leach out of the mixture. **Do not discard** (my grandmother's stern but sage words). Skim the fat and keep it in a small saucepan to warm up and drizzle over the porridge later.

Bring the milk to a simmer in a fresh medium pan, making sure not to burn it, and then add it to the pan containing the skimmed porridge. Stir the milky porridge mix constantly over a low-medium heat for 5 minutes until the consistency looks even. Stir in the salt and caster sugar, sample the mix and then add further salt or sugar to taste. The porridge should have a pronounced tang from the cream, but it shouldn't taste bland.

Serve hot in warmed bowls. To finish, drizzle the *rømmegrøt* with the warm sour cream fat and sprinkle more caster sugar and cinnamon to taste. Enjoy the creamy, tangy porridge and be prepared to sleep like a baby!

Dessert

Dessert

Whenever I think of dessert, the word that springs to mind is *lettvint*, the Norwegian term for easy. I am a firm believer in fuss-free desserts, something you can whip together with a handful of great ingredients and a little preparation. Scandinavian desserts tend to be seasonal, with a bias towards light fruit dishes in the summer and indulgent creamy puddings in the winter – but ice cream and chocolate brownies are firm favourites all year round.

You'll spot the Nordic love of summer berries in these recipes, from strawberry snow to fruity sorbets and blackcurrant ice cream. There are simple desserts for elegant suppers, like berries with white chocolate sauce or wonderfully wobbly lingonberry jelly, as well as traditional puddings like apple and rye trifle, cherry soup and Scandinavian vanilla rice pudding. Or why not have a go at making your own ice cream cornets or playing around with different jelly flavours for something more exciting than the everyday?

There are also scrumptious treats such as Valhalla cherry brownies, a Norwegian twist on the classic cheesecake (complete with tipsy strawberries) and a devilishly good *Daim* sundae. As we say in Norway, *velbekomme*!

The secret to making ice cream without a freezer
Strawberry sorbet
Fruit of the forest and star anise sorbet
Blackcurrant ice cream
Banana and cardamom ice cream
Lemon and nutmeg *krumkaker* (ice cream cornets)
Daim caramel sauce
Daim and clotted cream ice cream sundae
Tilslørte bondepiker (Scandinavian apple and rye trifle)
Mansikkalumi (Finnish strawberry snow)
Sour cherry soup
Iced Nordic berries with white chocolate and cardamom sauce
Norwegian cheesecake with tipsy strawberries
Risengrynsgrøt (Scandinavian vanilla rice pudding)
Valhalla brownies
The secret to making jelly
Lingonberry jelly with macerated strawberries

The secret to making ice cream without a freezer

In each of the frozen dessert recipes below, I have included the two 'standard' ways of freezing ice cream and sorbet – either using an ice cream machine or by hand using a freezer. However, if you're feeling adventurous there is a rather cool third way, based on the method used long before freezers were invented.

Create your own 'freezing mixture' by putting 1kg of crushed ice in a large plastic washing bowl, then adding 200g salt dissolved in 300ml water. The salt lowers the temperature of the ice and creates an instant ice bath for freezing your sorbet or custard mixture, which is ideal as the faster it freezes, the better the texture will be. Pour your mixture in a metal baking tin and float the tin in the ice bath, making sure that you don't get any salty water in your mixture. Carefully stir the mixture and scrape the bottom of the baking tin with a fork every few minutes to circulate the cooler liquid from the bottom and break up the ice crystals forming there. Within 30 minutes you should have perfectly smooth sorbet or ice cream, ready to serve straight from the tin!

Strawberry sorbet

Sorbets are always a crowd pleaser, especially after a heavy meal. I like to serve them just as they are, unembellished, letting their icy flavours take central stage. Strawberry sorbet, made when the berries are at their plumpest juiciest best, is the most romantic of summer desserts. I find that it is worth making up the sugar syrup in advance, since it keeps well in the fridge for a few weeks, and chilled syrup results in a smoother sorbet. I use orange liqueur in this sorbet to add a subtle citrussy tone and to make it slightly softer, but if you'd rather not, you can either simply omit it, or replace it with a couple of tablespoons of sugar syrup infused with orange zest instead.

SERVES 8

250g fructose (or 375g caster sugar)
150ml water
800g strawberries, hulled

juice of 1 lemon
2 tbsp Grand Marnier (or Cointreau)
2 medium egg whites, lightly whisked

Bring the fructose and water to a simmer in a small pan, and allow the sugar to dissolve for 2-3 minutes over a low heat. Set aside to cool completely before using. If you want to speed the cooling process, pour the syrup in a small bowl (preferably metal) and float that bowl in a larger bowl (or sinkful) of iced water.

Blitz the strawberries, lemon juice and Grand Marnier in a blender until smooth. Add 150-200ml of the syrup and blitz again. Taste to check the sweetness and add more syrup if necessary – the mixture should be slightly sweeter than you want the final sorbet to be, as it will taste less sweet once frozen. If there's any syrup left over, keep it in a sealed bottle or jar in the fridge and use for sweetening drinks or other sorbet recipes.

Pour the strawberry purée in to a large bowl, add the whisked egg whites and mix until thoroughly combined. You can then use the 'freezing mixture' method (opposite), an ice cream maker or a freezer to make your sorbet.

If you have an ice cream maker, pour the sorbet mixture in and churn for 20-30 minutes, depending on your ice cream machine, until the sorbet holds its shape when you scoop it in to a soft ball.

If you're using a freezer, pour the sorbet mix in to a freezer-proof bowl or box and put it in the freezer for a couple of hours, taking it out every 15 minutes or so to stir well with a fork. Make sure that you bring the sorbet in from the edges and mix through – this will break up the ice crystals starting to form on the perimeter and distribute the cooler mixture from the edges throughout the sorbet so that you get an even 'freeze'. Allow a few hours for this – you want to keep breaking up those ice crystals while the mixture freezes, in order to give the finished sorbet a smooth, scoopable consistency. If the sorbet does end up freezing rather solid, you can always put chunks of the frozen mixture in a blender or food processor and blitz to a nice smooth sorbet consistency.

Serve immediately or store in the freezer in a lidded container until needed.

Fruit of the forest and star anise sorbet

I use a mixture of raspberries, blueberries, redcurrants, blackcurrants and blackberries for this sorbet, but feel free to use only some of these or to substitute cherries or strawberries, as the fancy takes you. Adding the alcohol gives this sweet sorbet a subtle little kick and also keeps it slightly softer than plain fruit sorbets. Do feel free to use a different liqueur or to omit the alcohol altogether if you'd rather.

SERVES 8

250g fructose (or 375g caster sugar)
150ml water
5 star anise
1 long cinnamon stick
 (or 2 smaller ones)
2 long peels of lemon zest
800g mixed fruit of the forest
 (fresh or frozen)
juice of ½ lemon
2 tbsp aquavit, sambuca or vodka
2 medium egg whites,
 lightly whisked

Bring the fructose and water to a simmer in a small pan and allow the sugar to dissolve for 2-3 minutes over a low heat. Remove the pan from the heat, add the spices and lemon zest to the hot syrup and leave to infuse for 30 minutes. Set the syrup to one side to cool completely before using. If you want to speed the cooling process, pour the syrup in a small bowl (preferably metal) and float that bowl in a larger bowl (or sinkful) of iced water. Do remember to remove the spices and zest from the cooled syrup before using it in the sorbet mixture.

Blitz the berries, lemon juice and alcohol in a blender until smooth. Add 150-200ml of the syrup and blitz again. Taste to check the sweetness and add more syrup if necessary – the mixture should be slightly sweeter than you want the final sorbet to be, as it will taste less sweet once frozen. If there's any syrup left over, keep it in a sealed bottle or jar in the fridge and use for sweetening drinks or other sorbet recipes.

If you don't mind berry pips in your sorbet, simply pour the berry purée in to a large bowl, add the whisked egg whites and mix until thoroughly combined. If you prefer your sorbet pip-free, push the purée through a fine sieve or chinois before mixing with the egg whites. You can then use the 'freezing mixture' method (page 182, Desserts), an ice cream maker or a freezer to make your sorbet.

If you have an ice cream maker, churn the sorbet mixture for 20-30 minutes (depending on your machine) until the sorbet holds its shape when you scoop it in to a soft ball.

Alternatively, put the sorbet mix in a freezer-proof box or bowl in the freezer for a couple of hours, taking out to stir well with a fork every 15 minutes or so, bringing the ice crystals in from the edges and mixing through to get an even 'freeze'. You need to keep breaking up the ice while the mix freezes for a smooth, scoopable finished sorbet. If it does freeze solid, you can always blitz chunks to a smooth consistency in a blender or food processor.

Serve immediately or store in the freezer in a lidded container until needed.

Blackcurrant ice cream

Most Scandinavians would agree that really good ice cream is a thing of beauty. It doesn't seem to matter how cold it is outside, they always seem to have room in their hearts (and stomachs) for ice cream. This is an adaptation of food scientist Peter Barham's basic custard and cream ice cream recipe. I usually prepare the custard the night before making the ice cream, as chilling it helps improve the consistency of the ice cream. If you can't get hold of blackcurrants, try blackberries, raspberries or mulberries which all work wonderfully.

SERVES 8

250g fresh or frozen blackcurrants

50g fructose (or 75g caster sugar)

4 medium egg yolks

500ml milk

100g sugar (or 60g fructose)

300ml whipping cream

Blitz the blackcurrants with the fructose in a blender to make a simple blackcurrant purée.

Whisk the egg yolks with the milk and sugar, then pour in a medium saucepan. Put the pan over a moderate to low heat and stir the thin milky liquid constantly with a wooden spoon until you see it begin to thicken. This will take between 5 and 10 minutes, depending how low you keep the heat. Once it is thick enough to coat the back of a spoon and separates to leave a line if you run your finger through the coating, you've got custard (if you want to be a little more scientific, then invest in a thermometer and stir until it reaches 78°C). As soon as the custard is ready, take the saucepan off the heat and allow the custard to cool completely before refrigerating for at least an hour, or preferably overnight. Make sure that the custard is completely chilled before freezing as otherwise the texture of the finished ice cream can be rather grainy.

When you're ready to make the ice cream, add the fruit purée and cream to the chilled custard and stir well to combine. You can then use the 'freezing mixture' method (page 182, Desserts), an ice cream maker or a freezer to make your ice cream.

If you have an ice cream maker, pour the custard mixture in and churn for 30 minutes or so, until the ice cream is smooth and velvety.

If you're using a freezer, pour the custard mixture in to a freezer-proof bowl or box and put it in the freezer for a couple of hours, taking it out every 15 minutes or so to stir well with a fork. Make sure that you bring the freezing custard in from the edges and stir through – this will break up the ice crystals starting to form on the perimeter and distribute the cooler mixture throughout the ice cream so that you get an even 'freeze'. Allow a few hours for this – you want to keep breaking up those ice crystals while the mixture freezes, in order to give the finished ice cream a smooth, scoopable consistency.

Serve immediately or store in the freezer in a lidded container until needed.

Banana and cardamom ice cream

My mother would make banana ice cream for me as a childhood birthday treat. It remains my favourite ice cream and I have yet to try a better version anywhere. Although we ate this as a pure banana ice cream as children, I think that the subtle cardamom flavour adds a little extra something. Feel free to substitute grated nutmeg or ground cinnamon or clove if you fancy a different flavour combination. If you're making this for children, you may wish to omit the alcohol.

SERVES 4-6

300ml whipping cream
1 tsp freshly ground cardamom
4 small ripe bananas
50g fructose (or 75g caster sugar), plus more to taste
1 tbsp rum or brandy
pinch of salt

Put the cream and ground cardamom in a small saucepan, bring to a simmer and cook for 1-2 minutes before removing from the heat. Allow to infuse for 30 minutes and cool completely.

Once the cream has cooled, blitz the bananas and fructose in a blender or mash together by hand. Add the cardamom-infused cream, alcohol and salt to the sweetened banana and either blitz or mash together, as appropriate. Taste to check the sweetness and add more fructose if necessary – the mixture should be slightly sweeter than you want the final ice cream to be, as it will taste less sweet once frozen. You can then use the 'freezing mixture' method (page 182, Desserts), an ice cream maker or a freezer to make your ice cream.

If you have an ice cream maker, pour the banana mixture in and churn for 20-30 minutes, until the ice cream is smooth and velvety.

If you're using a freezer, pour the ice cream mixture in to a freezer-proof bowl or box and put it in the freezer for a couple of hours, taking it out every 15 minutes or so to stir well with a fork. Make sure that you bring the freezing banana cream in from the edges and stir through – this will break up the ice crystals starting to form on the perimeter and distribute the cooler mixture throughout the ice cream so that you get an even 'freeze'. Allow a few hours for this – you want to keep breaking up those ice crystals while the mixture freezes, in order to give the finished ice cream a smooth, scoopable consistency.

Serve immediately or store in the freezer in a lidded container until needed.

Lemon and nutmeg *krumkaker* (ice cream cornets)

The krumkake (cornet) iron is a classic piece of Scandinavian cooking kit, ideal for making the most delicious, crispy ice cream cones. If you get the chance to buy a cornet iron, I heartily recommend that you do so – it's enormous fun to use. However, don't worry if you haven't got one as these krumkaker can also be baked in the oven like brandy snaps. The secret to getting a really professional-looking cornet shape is to wrap the sides together very quickly while the krumkake is still warm. You can always make vanilla cones by replacing the lemon zest and nutmeg with a teaspoon or so of vanilla extract, or try using orange zest or different spices to complement the ice cream or sorbet that you'll be putting in them.

MAKES 10-12

1 medium egg	3 tbsp water
110g sugar	zest of 1 lemon
110g plain flour	½ tsp freshly grated nutmeg
110g butter, melted	pinch of salt

Plug in your *krumkake* iron to heat up, or preheat the oven to 190°C/170°C fan/gas mark 5 and prepare a baking sheet with parchment or greaseproof paper.

If you are oven baking the cornets, I recommend making a stencil-type template out of something durable (and washable!) like an old plastic ice cream tub lid, so that your cornets will be a uniform size. Draw a circle roughly 20cm in diameter on the lid. Then draw a square outside the circle, leaving at least 1-2cm between the edge of the circle and the sides of the square. Use a sharp-bladed box cutter or stationery knife to cut along the edges of the square and then cut the circle out of the middle, creating a square stencil with a round hole in it.

Whisk the egg and sugar together in a medium bowl until pale and fluffy and then gradually whisk in the flour, butter and water a little at a time. Add the zest, nutmeg and salt before beating everything together until there are no lumps. It should form a very thick batter.

Krumkake iron: Brush the heated *krumkake* iron cooking surfaces with melted butter (or wipe with a bit of buttered kitchen paper) and place a tablespoonful of the mixture in a dollop on the bottom heating plate. Close the lid and cook for 3-4 minutes depending on how hot the iron gets (you want the cooked cornets to be no browner than a light caramel colour or they may scorch).

Oven baking: Starting at one corner of your lined baking sheet, put your stencil on the sheet and dollop about a tablespoonful of mixture on the bit of baking sheet showing through the hole. Holding the stencil firmly in place with one hand, use a palette knife to spread the cornet mixture out to cover the exposed circle of baking sheet with an even layer roughly 2-3mm thick. Then carefully lift your stencil and scrape any excess mixture left on it back in to the bowl, so that none gets wasted. You should now have a perfect circle of cornet mixture on your baking sheet, and a clean stencil ready to be used to make the next cornet. The mixture doesn't spread much when it cooks so you can pack your circles quite close together across and down the baking sheet until it is full. Bake on the upper shelf of the oven for 5-7 minutes or until light caramel brown (no darker in case they scorch).

Once cooked, you need to shape each *krumkake* in to the traditional cornet shape while still warm and pliable, being careful not to burn your fingers! It may seem rather fiddly at first, but you'll quickly get the knack. I find that the best method is to bend the warm *krumkake* quickly in to a simple cone and then to stand it (pointy end downwards) in an empty glass or a cup, so it holds its shape while cooling.

The cones can be made in advance and stored in an airtight container for a week or so until needed. When you come to use them, simply pop them in the oven at 150°C/130°C fan/gas mark 2 for 5 minutes to give them a little extra crispiness.

Daim caramel sauce

This is an adaptation of a lemon thyme caramel recipe by London chocolatier
Paul A Young. I've omitted the herb so that the Daim *bar can take centre stage, but by all*
means experiment with flavouring your caramel with aromatic herbs like rosemary or
mint, or perhaps a pinch of chilli flakes. If you can't get hold of Milka Daim *chocolate, use*
one Daim *bar broken into pieces and mixed with a heaped teaspoon of cocoa powder instead.*

MAKES AROUND 500G SAUCE

150g unsalted butter
150g light muscovado sugar
10g sea salt
150ml double cream
50g Milka *Daim* chocolate, chopped

Melt the butter in a large saucepan, add the sugar and stir until dissolved. Bring to
the boil and simmer for 5 minutes before stirring the salt in until dissolved.

Remove the pan from the heat and add the cream, standing back as it can splutter
and spit at this stage. Whisk well until all the cream is incorporated. Add the
Milka *Daim* chocolate and mix until fully melted. Serve hot if using straight away,
or allow to cool and then store for up to 2 months in the fridge in an airtight jar.

VARIATIONS

* If you're in the mood for something spicy, try adding cardamom pods, cinnamon,
star anise, nutmeg or cloves with the cream to infuse it – but do remember to sieve
them out before using the sauce!

* If you're feeling Scandinavian, substitute 50g of Norwegian brown cheese for
the milk chocolate for a sweet-savoury salt caramel type sauce. I promise you won't
be disappointed…

* If you're a fan of Scandinavian salted liquorice, why not chop up 50g and melt it
in around 25ml of water in a pan, to add to the caramel instead of the chocolate.
I would recommend omitting the salt from the caramel mix in this case, as the salty
liquorice should provide enough on its own – but obviously it depends on what
liquorice you use, so do taste the finished sauce and stir in 5g or so of salt if you think
it needs it.

Daim and clotted cream ice cream sundae

Ice cream sundaes are delightfully indulgent and easy to compose – you simply use your favourite ice cream, embellish with whatever fruit or sweets you have to hand and drizzle your favourite syrup or sauce over the lot. This is one of my favourite combinations. I like to let the Daim *caramel sauce (opposite) and chocolate take the spotlight by using a simple clotted cream ice cream base, rather than a stronger flavour like vanilla.*

SERVES 4

12 scoops clotted cream ice cream
1 pack *Daim* balls or 1 large *Daim* bar broken in to bite-size pieces
100g toasted almonds, crushed
Daim caramel sauce (c. 50-100ml per person)

Simply divide the ice cream between four sundae glasses, scatter the chocolate and almonds over the top, drizzle with *Daim* caramel sauce and serve with a wicked smile.

Tilslørte bondepiker
(Scandinavian apple and rye trifle)

This is a traditional pudding, known by a variety of different names throughout Scandinavia. These range from the prosaic Danish 'apple cake' (æblekage) to the heavenly-sounding Swedish 'angel's food' (änglamat) and the thoroughly bizarre Norwegian 'veiled farm girls' (tilslørte bondepiker)! The unusual combination of apple, cream and rye bread works so well – the apples are just sweet enough and fragrant with cinnamon, while the caramelised breadcrumbs add crunch and flavour – and it is much fresher-tasting than traditional trifles. I like the cooked apples to be quite tart to cut through the creamy layers, but do feel free to add more fructose or sugar to the apple mix when cooking if you prefer a sweeter compote. If you want to whip this dessert up in a hurry, you could use 200g of sweet 'n' crispy rye granola (page 21, Breakfast) instead of the caramelised rye bread crumbs.

SERVES 8

8 large cooking apples, peeled and chopped
2 tsp cinnamon
150g fructose (or 225g caster sugar)
125ml water
200g stale (or dried) dark rye bread

75g butter
300ml double cream
300ml crème fraiche
1 tsp vanilla extract
4 tbsp fructose (or 6 tbsp caster sugar)
100g almonds, toasted and crushed

Put the apple pieces in a large saucepan and sprinkle with the cinnamon and 100g of the fructose. Add the water and simmer gently for 15 minutes or so over a medium heat until the apples break down and most of the water evaporates.

Meanwhile blitz the rye bread in a blender until it is the consistency of rough breadcrumbs. Dry fry the rye crumbs in a large sauté pan for 2 minutes, then add the remaining 50g of fructose along with the butter and a pinch of salt and fry for another 2-3 minutes until you can smell a sweet, nutty caramelised smell. Allow the breadcrumbs to cool before assembling the dish.

Lightly whip the cold double cream and crème fraiche with the vanilla extract and 4 tablespoons of fructose in a large bowl until soft peaks form.

This dish looks best served in individual glasses – try using heavy whisky tumblers or pretty martini glasses. Place a dollop of cooled apple compote in each glass, then a layer of caramelised rye crumbs, followed by a layer of whipped cream. Repeat the layering process, finishing with a layer of cream and scattering the toasted almonds on top. Chill for 1 hour before serving.

Mansikkalumi
(Finnish strawberry snow)

This is a great dessert for long, languid summer evenings spent with friends in the garden or on the terrace. If you prefer, you can always substitute whipping cream for crème fraiche. Make sure the cream is cold before you whip it, as this ensures a more billowing result.

SERVES 6

200ml crème fraiche
600g strawberries, hulled, plus extra to garnish
50-80g fructose (or 75-120g caster sugar)
2 tbsp Grand Marnier (optional)
4 egg whites

Whip the cold crème fraiche in a large bowl until peaks start to form and then refrigerate while you prepare the rest of the ingredients. Blitz the strawberries in a blender (or mash with a fork in a bowl) with 50g of the fructose. Taste for sweetness and add as much of the remaining fructose as you think the mixture needs (remember that the strawberry flavour will be slightly diluted by the egg white and whipped crème fraiche, so you may want to make it slighter sweeter than normal). Add the Grand Marnier (if using) to the sweetened strawberry purée.

Beat the egg whites with a pinch of salt in a separate bowl until stiff peaks form. Remove the whipped crème fraiche from the fridge and fold the strawberry purée in to it with a large metal spoon. Pour this creamy strawberry mixture in to the beaten egg whites and gently fold through until all the ingredients are incorporated, taking care not to knock all the air out.

Scoop the strawberry snow into glass bowls or goblets, cover with clingfilm and refrigerate until you're ready to serve. It will only keep for a few hours in the fridge so don't be tempted to make this a day in advance! Decorate with whole or halved strawberries before serving, then dig in.

Sour cherry soup

Fruit soups are a Scandinavian favourite and they make a fantastic chilled dessert for kids and adults alike. You can use pretty much any summer fruit – blueberries, bilberries, raspberries, strawberries, rosehips, cherries, blackberries, plums and currants of all colours – either on its own or in combination with others. My grandparents had several kirsebær, *or sour cherry, trees on their farm and we loved eating this tart, ruby-coloured, intensely flavourful fruit as stunning crimson summer soup. If you can't lay your hands on any fresh sour cherries, then make this with sweet cherries spiked with the juice of one lemon and only use 25-35g of fructose (40-50g caster sugar).*

SERVES 2-4

500g sour cherries, washed and pitted, plus extra to garnish
300ml water
50g fructose (or 75g caster sugar), plus more to taste
100ml cherry liqueur
2 tbsp cornstarch (optional)
4 heaped tbsp sour cream

Bring the sour cherries and water to a simmer in a large saucepan and cook over a low heat for 5-10 minutes until the cherries break up and start to look mushy. Add the fructose and liqueur, stir thoroughly and simmer again for 5 minutes until the fructose has dissolved.

Blitz in a blender and taste, adding more fructose if you think it needs it. If the consistency seems a little watery, pour the cherry purée back in the pan and bring to a simmer. Mix the cornstarch with two tablespoons of water and whisk in to the simmering sour cherry soup. Cook for a further 2-3 minutes until the soup thickens.

Chill the soup for a couple of hours and then serve either just as it is or after sieving (if you prefer a smoother consistency). Finish with a dollop of sour cream.

Iced Nordic berries with white chocolate and cardamom sauce

This is my Scandi take on one of the signature dishes at The Ivy restaurant in London. It is simple, pretty, delicious, easy to prepare. I think cardamom and white chocolate is a match made in heaven, but if you'd rather, you can omit the cardamom and use a splash of vanilla extract or a few vanilla bean seeds instead. If you can't find vanilla salt in the shops, you can make it very simply by combining vanilla pod seeds with sea salt (one pod is enough for about 225g salt), which can then be stored in an airtight jar with the scraped pod for extra flavour. Do make sure the berries are frozen before starting this dish as it takes less than 10 minutes to prepare!

SERVES 6

12 cardamom pods
500ml double cream
400g white chocolate, broken
small pinch of vanilla salt
600g frozen sour cherries, blueberries, blackcurrants,
    redcurrants, raspberries and blackberries

Gently open the cardamom pods by applying gentle pressure using a pestle and mortar or lightly squashing with a rolling pin. Bring the double cream and the opened cardamom pods to a simmer in a medium saucepan and continue to simmer over a low heat for 5 minutes to allow the spice to infuse. Put the white chocolate in a large heatproof bowl on a saucepan containing a couple of centimetres of simmering water over a low heat. Add the cardamom-infused cream and vanilla salt and stir until the chocolate melts.

Remove the berries from the freezer and distribute equally between 6 tall martini glasses or shallow bowls. Pour the hot white chocolate cardamom sauce over the berries and serve immediately.

Norwegian cheesecake with tipsy strawberries

This is a classic New York cheesecake but the base is made with Scandinavian pepperkaker *or ginger biscuits. You could use digestive biscuits if you prefer. Take the cream and cheese out of the fridge an hour or so before starting to make the cheesecake, as they will mix better at room temperature.*

SERVES 8

Base
200g *pepperkaker* or
  ginger biscuit crumbs
50g melted butter
50g demerara sugar
pinch of ground cinnamon

Filling
4 eggs, separated
175g caster sugar
240ml sour cream
1 tsp vanilla
2 tbsp plain flour
240g full-fat cream cheese

Tipsy strawberries
40g cold unsalted butter
2 punnets strawberries
  (hulled and halved
  or quartered)
3 tbsp brandy
3 tbsp Grand Marnier
juice of 2-3 oranges
zest of 1 orange

Preheat the oven to 160°C/140°C fan/gas mark 3. Lightly oil a 23cm round cake tin and set aside. Mix the cheesecake base ingredients in a medium bowl with a pinch of salt, then tip them into the base of the cake tin, press down firmly and refrigerate.

Beat the egg yolks in a large bowl with 125g sugar until pale, then add the sour cream, vanilla, flour and a pinch of salt. Beat in the cream cheese a large spoonful at a time.

Beat the egg whites separately with the remaining 50g of sugar until stiff peaks form. Add one large spoonful of this to the cheesecake mixture to loosen it, then fold through the rest of the egg whites, being careful not to knock out all the air.

Spoon the mixture into the chilled cake tin, flatten the top with a pallet knife and bake in the middle of the oven for 45-50 minutes, or until the surface feels firm. Cheesecake shouldn't take on too much colour, so check after 25 minutes and if necessary turn the heat down 20° or so. Leave to cool in the oven for an hour after turning the oven off.

Melt half the butter in a large sauté pan, add the strawberries and sear for 1-2 minutes until they soften. Add the brandy and Grand Marnier, stir and allow the alcohol to evaporate for 1-2 minutes. Flambé the berries if you're confident that it won't set the kitchen on fire! Remove the berries with a slotted spoon and set aside, then add the orange juice and zest to the pan and heat to reduce the liquid by half. Add the remaining cold butter to add gloss to the sauce before stirring the strawberries back in.

Drizzle a large spoonful of warm tipsy strawberries over each slice of cooled cheesecake and serve.

Risengrynsgrøt
(Scandinavian vanilla rice pudding)

Grøt or porridge is often eaten in Norway instead of a savoury evening meal. It is a treat on chilly winter evenings when you're curled up on the sofa reading or watching TV. Grøt can be made with oats, rye, wheat, barley or, as in this instance, rice. I've kept this recipe deliberately low on sugar to contrast with a sweet topping, but if you like sweet rice pudding, you may wish to add a few more tablespoons of sugar while cooking. I love this dish topped with a pat of butter, a sprinkle of crunchy demerara sugar and a liberal dusting of cinnamon, but this pudding is also fantastic with cooked plums or plum jam (page 16, Breakfast). If you want to jazz it up a bit further, add spices and some orange zest to the milk, or try making it with coconut milk, or even adding some cocoa or chocolate for a truly decadent chocolate rice pudding!

SERVES 6-8

300g pudding or arborio (risotto) rice
2 tbsp butter
½ tsp salt
1 litre whole milk
1 tsp vanilla extract
1 tbsp sugar (or more to taste)

Rinse the rice under cold water in a sieve and allow to drain. Bring 600ml of water to the boil in a large saucepan, then add the rice, butter and salt. Cook on a medium heat for 10 minutes until the rice has absorbed all the water, stirring occasionally so that it doesn't clump together at the bottom of the pan.

Add the milk, vanilla and sugar and bring to the boil stirring constantly for a few minutes. Then turn the heat right down low to a gentle simmer. Unlike risotto you won't have to babysit the rice, but do give it an occasional stir while it slowly cooks over the next 30 minutes.

It is ready to serve once it has thickened to the point where it takes a few seconds to drop off a spoon. Pour in to large cereal bowls and finish with a sweet topping – butter, sugar and cinnamon or jam, fruit compote, golden syrup, treacle or honey – the choice is yours!

Any you don't eat can be stored in the fridge and eaten hot or cold the next day. If you're eating it cold, you may wish to stir in some whipped vanilla cream or crème fraiche to stop it being too stodgy, as it will have congealed somewhat as it cools.

Valhalla brownies

All too often I find myself daydreaming about American brownies, the kind that are chewy and mallowy without being too sweet. These are my Scandi version with liqueur-drenched sour cherries lending a welcome tartness to the intense chocolate hit.

MAKES 12

100g dried sour cherries
3-4 tbsp cherry liqueur
juice of ½ lemon
125g butter
200g dark chocolate,
  broken into small pieces

4 tbsp cocoa powder
3 medium eggs
110g golden caster sugar
110g icing sugar
1 tsp vanilla extract
150g refined spelt (or plain) flour

Preheat the oven to 180°C/160°C fan/gas mark 4. Line a 20cm square baking tin or brownie tin with two sheets of parchment paper laid over each other at 90° to form a cross in the base (this makes it easier to remove the cooked brownies without squashing them).

Put the dried cherries, cherry liqueur and lemon juice in a small bowl, stir well, cover and leave to soak for at least an hour (or overnight).

Put the butter, chocolate and cocoa powder in a heatproof bowl and position it on top of a saucepan containing a couple of centimetres of simmering water. Allow everything to melt over a low heat and stir with a spatula once in a while.

Whisk the eggs, sugars and vanilla extract in a separate large bowl. Add the melted chocolate mixture and stir thoroughly, then tip in the flour and combine well. Drain the sour cherries (keep the liqueur for drizzling on ice cream or other desserts) and stir them in too.

Pour the brownie mixture in to the prepared tin and bake on the middle shelf of the oven for 25-30 minutes. Keep an eye on them as the secret to cooking brownies is to undercook them slightly. If they bake for too long, they lose some of their intense chocolate flavour and become crumbly and dry. I find that the best way to check that they are sufficiently cooked is to pat the top of the mixture – it should feel dry but not firm. You can also check by inserting a skewer in to the middle of the brownies: there should be a little bit of uncooked mixture left on it when you pull it out.

Remove from the oven and leave to cool in the tin on a wire rack. Once they've cooled completely, you can slice them and remove from the tin. If you store them in a sealed container in the fridge, the texture goes really firm and they'll keep for up to a week – provided you can resist scoffing them all in one sitting, that is!

The secret to making jelly

Jelly is a wonderful light dessert to enjoy at any time of the day, any season of the year. It's clean and delicious to round off a quiet supper at home or as a little something sweet at the end of a dinner party. It slips down beautifully all on its own; it's fabulous with a generous dollop of whipped cream perched precariously on top; and my Norwegian grandmother would serve it with cold vanilla custard – heavenly!

The secret to making jelly is to remember the basic formula: one leaf of gelatine to set 100ml of liquid. However, jellies made in a mould – which have to be able to stand on their own – need more gelatine than jellies set and served in a glass, bowl or cup, which can be a bit wobblier. For moulded jellies, I use 4½ leaves of gelatine to set 450ml of liquid, whereas I find that 4 leaves are sufficient to set 450ml of liquid for unmoulded jelly.

My favourite no-fuss way to make jelly is to use high-fruit cordials. Why not try serving fresh or macerated strawberries with elderflower cordial jelly? Or rose cordial jelly topped with fresh or candied edible flowers? Blackcurrant cordial jelly with fresh blueberries? Or lemon cordial jelly garnished with lemon verbena or mint? Just follow the general method below and substitute your cordial for the lingonberry one. I tend to use the cordial quite concentrated in jellies – roughly 1 part cordial to 3 parts water – but it is safest to taste first to check how strong or dilute the cordial is, as strengths vary from brand to brand.

Jelly is versatile, fun and easy to make – so what are you waiting for? Stock up on gelatine and start experimenting!

Lingonberry jelly
with macerated strawberries

Given the Scandinavian love of berries, it seems only right and proper to conclude with a recipe for lingonberry jelly and fruity liqueur-soaked strawberries. The simple jelly-berry combination makes a deliciously refreshing end to a meal, either on its own or with a dollop of something creamy on top for a summery treat. You could even balance a scoop of vanilla ice cream on the boozy berries, for an alcoholic take on the childhood favourite, jelly and ice cream. Try macerating different fresh or frozen fruit to accompany the jelly – cherries, raspberries and blackberries all work brilliantly with lingonberry – and using different liqueurs (orange ones like Grand Marnier and Cointreau always go beautifully with strawberries), or feel free to omit the alcohol altogether if you want sober strawberries instead. Finally, if you fancy a real treat, I recommend following in my grandmother's footsteps and eating your jelly with lashings of hot or cold vanilla custard!

This recipe works on the basis that you will be setting the jelly in glasses or small bowls to serve and therefore uses 4-4½ leaves of gelatine to 500ml of liquid (depending how wobbly you like your jelly). If you want to make it in a mould to turn out instead, you will need to increase the gelatine to 5 leaves so that the jelly will be firm enough to stand on its own.

SERVES 4

Jelly
125 ml lingonberry cordial
  (or more to taste)
375ml water
4-4½ leaves gelatine

Macerated strawberries
20g cold unsalted butter
1 punnet strawberries
  (hulled and quartered)
1 tbsp brandy
2 tbsp Chambord (or Crème de Cassis
  or Framboise) liqueur
juice of 2 oranges
zest of 1 orange
whipped cream, crème fraiche
  or vanilla ice cream
  to finish (optional)

Mix the cordial and water in a jug and taste to see how sweet (and how strongly flavoured) it is. The cordial-water mix should be somewhat sweeter than you want the finished jelly to be, as it will taste less sweet once refrigerated and set. Add more cordial if required, then measure out 500ml of the mixture to use in the jelly. If you've added more cordial, you will have some left over to use in drinks later. Don't be tempted to use more than 500ml for the jelly, as it won't set properly.

Cut the gelatine leaves in to thirds or quarters and place in a heatproof bowl. Add a few tablespoons of the cordial mixture – just enough to cover the the gelatine – and leave for 10 minutes to soften.

Bring a small pan of water to a simmer and place the bowl of softened gelatine over the simmering water. Heat the gelatine until it has totally melted and then add the remainder of the cordial mixture, stirring to combine.

Pour the jelly mix through a sieve in to a jug and from this, carefully pour in to the glasses or small bowls (remembering to leave enough room at the top for a layer of berries). Pop them in the fridge to set for at least 2-3 hours, and preferably more.

Melt half the butter in a sauté pan, add the strawberries and sear for 1-2 minutes until they soften. Add the brandy and Chambord, stir and allow the alcohol to evaporate for 1-2 minutes. Flambé the berries if you're confident that it won't set the kitchen on fire! Remove the berries with a slotted spoon and set aside on a small plate, then add the orange juice and zest to the pan and heat to reduce the liquid by half. Add the remaining butter to gloss the sauce before stirring the strawberries back in. Leave to cool.

Just before serving, remove the jellies from the fridge and spoon a generous layer of the macerated strawberries on to each one. Serve just as it is or top with a large spoonful of whipped cream or crème fraiche or a scoop of vanilla ice cream.

Sig's Scandi Store Cupboard and Suppliers

You may find it helpful to have some pointers on where to find the more unusual ingredients in this book, like apple vinegar with lingonberries or rosehip syrup, and to know who (in my opinion) makes the best sourdough crispbread on the planet or which are my preferred brands of spelt flour, bio yoghurt or my beloved brown cheese.

I've compiled a list of Scandi specialties and Signe favourites, along with some suggestions of where you can find them if they aren't widely available. In general I find that between Waitrose, IKEA, local delicatessens and websites like www.danishfooddirect.co.uk, www.totallyswedish.com and www.scandikitchen.co.uk, I can get hold of the majority of the items listed below.

Aalborg Jubilæums Akvavit
(www.danishfooddirect.co.uk)

Abba anchovies (IKEA)

Atkins & Potts rosehip syrup (Lakeland)

A. Vogel Herbamare salt (health food shops)

Belvoir, Bottle Green or Waitrose
elderflower cordial

Billington's natural sugar crystals and
other sugars

Chocolate by Trish cooking chocolate
(www.chocolatebytrish.com or
Selfridges)

Court Lodge Organic Bio Pouring
Yoghurt (Abel & Cole)

Crispy fried onions (www.danishfooddirect.
co.uk and www.totallyswedish.com)

Forman & Field smoked & cured salmon
(Waitrose)

Gorwydd Caerphilly cheese (Waitrose)

Halen Môn smoked sea salt and vanilla
salt (www.seasalt.co.uk or Waitrose)

IKEA Food apple vinegar with
lingonberries

IKEA Food pickled herring fillets

Jordan's country crisp cereal

Jess's Ladies Organic unhomogenised whole
milk (health food shops)

Kelly's clotted cream ice cream
(Sainsbury's and Waitrose)

Kraft Daim bars and Daim balls (IKEA

and www.totallyswedish.com)

Krisprolls (www.totallyswedish.com)

Marigold powdered vegetable stock

Milka milk chocolate with Daim
(Sainsbury's and Waitrose)

Mills Kaviar (Scandinavian Kitchen
deli – London)

Peter's Yard sourdough crispbread
(www.petersyard.com)

Pixley Berries blackcurrant cordial
(Waitrose)

Rachel's Organic plain whole milk yoghurt

Rude Health muesli (Waitrose)

Sharpham Park spelt flour
(www.sharphampark.com)

Shipton Mill spelt flour
(www.shipton-mill.com)

Thorncroft rosehip cordial (Waitrose)

Tillman's of Sweden lingonberry cordial
(www.goodnessdirect.co.uk)

Tine Gudbrandsalsost and ekte gjetost
brown cheese (Waitrose and Whole
Foods Market)

Tine Snøfrisk goat's cheese (Waitrose)

Trénel Fils Griotte cherry liqueur

Waitrose chicken pâté forestier

Willie's Supreme Cacao

Womersley lemon, basil, bay and juniper
vinegar (www.womersleyfoods.co.uk)

Yeo Valley plain whole milk yoghurt

The Scandi Kitchen

We were lucky to have lots of help sourcing kitchenware, crockery and linens to use in the photographs for this book, and at the end of the shoot we were very reluctant to pack up all the lovely things to return them!

There has been a real growth of interest in Nordic design in recent years, from rainbow-coloured Iittala glassware and boldly patterned Marimekko textiles to design classics like the Arne Jacobsen Egg chair. The simple, functional, pared-down style which has always been central to the Scandinavian home is now increasingly popular worldwide, and in the UK these are some of the suppliers who have tracked down the best examples of Scandi home-wares. Happy shopping!

95% DANISH
www.95percentdanish.co.uk

HUS & HEM
www.husandhem.co.uk,

ILLUSTRATED LIVING
www.illustratedliving.co.uk

SCANDI LIVING
www.scandiliving.com

SKANDIUM
www.skandium.com

CLOUDBERRY LIVING
www.cloudberryliving.co.uk

DESIGN HOUSE STOCKHOLM
www.designhousestockholm.com

LIZ NILSSON
www.liznilsson.com

MARIMEKKO
www.marimekko.com

KATRIN MOYE
www.katrinmoye.com

SUPERNICE
www.supernice.co.uk

NEW HOUSE TEXTILES
www.newhousetextiles.co.uk

Acknowledgements

Writing a cookbook is never a solitary process and a great many people are owed my eternal gratitude and thanks for their support, enthusiasm and constructive criticism.

My parents Jane and Jan top the list. Mama J's insistence that we ate together every evening was and still is a Johansen family ritual and I cannot thank my mother enough for teaching me the value of mealtimes as social bond. Dad's enthusiasm for travel was crucial to opening my eyes to other food cultures. Juliet Robertson-MacDonald and Oddny Solveig Vikesland Johansen, my respective British and Norwegian grandmothers, were brilliant cooks and I learned a lot from their wisdom and wizardry in the kitchen. Thanks to Sue and Jason Alexander, Amy and Lorne Somerville, and to Fraser and Lynda Reid, my surrogate family in New Hampshire, who have always given their unconditional support and been generous to a fault.

Thanks to Tom, for your love, strength and ability to wind me up and calm me down whenever the occasion called for it. Thank you to Annabel Merullo at PFD for sharing a love of Norwegian food.

Secrets of Scandinavian Cooking wouldn't be what it is without the combined talent, diligence and skill of the team who worked on the book: Elizabeth Hallett at the helm of Saltyard Books, along with Bryony Nowell, Kate Brunt, Ami Smithson, Debi Treloar and Polly Webb-Wilson – and all the other colleagues who helped to bring this book to life. Thank you all for working your magic.

To pals from Cambridge and beyond whose friendship and encouragement means more than they might realise: Kaitlin, Aaron, James, Mathieu, Ezra, Nina and Finnbar, Nadia, Mungo, Eleonoora, Sophie, Giles, Ana-Katarina, John, and Arabella. I'd also like to thank Dr Harry West at SOAS, where I studied for my Masters in Food Anthropology, for such an inspiring and academically rigorous programme.

I owe Heston Blumenthal, Kyle Connaughton and Otto Romer at the Fat Duck Experimental Kitchen a huge thank you for letting me play – I mean experiment – with food in Heston's lab! (I'm still kicking myself for not staying on when I had the chance). Adam Sanderson provided endless amusement and encouragement during those three months in Bray. I would never have dared apply for a position as chef stagiaire there without a wonderful year's diploma course from Leiths School of Food and Wine under my belt, and I thank Hannah Westcott for being a fantastic teacher.

The gourmet gals Fiona Beckett, Fiona Sims and Judy Joo have each been brilliant sources of advice and support in recent years. Fiona Beckett in particular is owed a very special thanks for being a tremendous mentor and friend.

Blogging and Twitter have been dynamic avenues for learning more about food, and it's thanks to a thoroughly switched-on food community, including Niamh Shields, Linda Williams, Camilla and Nick Barnard, Lucy Pope, Sarah Canet, Petra Barran, Kerstin Rodgers, Wendy Wilson-Bett, Ian and Christina Tencor, Simon Majumdar, Richard Bertinet, Dino Joannides, Tim Hayward, James Ramsden, and Rachel McCormack, that I am continuously entertained, inspired and more than a little chuffed at having landed this gig in food writing.

Index

Page references for photographs are in **bold**

allspice: baked eggs with anchovy and
   allspice 64
roast allspice chicken 165
almonds: blackberry, almond and cardamom
   cake 116, **117**
   Mor Monsen 119
   Toscakake 121
anchovies: baked eggs with anchovy and
   allspice 64
   egg and anchovy soldiers **34**, 35
   Janssons frestelse **162**, 163
apples: apple compote 13
   bircher muesli for spring and summer 22
   the Green Goddess **44**, 45
   Norwegian knickerbocker glory 48, **49**
   spiced apple cake 115
   tilslørte bondepiker 192
aquavit: Scandinavian Bloody Mary 42, **43**
arme riddere cinnamon toast with strawberries
   and cream 56, **57**
asparagus: Mama Johansen's vegetable
   soup 96, **97**
roast asparagus with Västerbotten cheese 60

bacon: crushed pea, bacon and tarragon
   smørbrød 91
   Nordic club sandwich **92**, 93
baked eggs with anchovy and allspice 64
baked trout in crème fraiche 156, **156**
bananas: banana and cardamom ice cream 187
   banana, coconut and chocolate milkshake 47
   and cinnamon crispbread 32, **33**
barley: pearl barley porridge 25
beetroots: beetroot and ginger soup 148, **149**
   chicken liver pâté with pickled beetroot
   smørbrød 90
   egg, beetroot and cottage cheese salad 101
   gravlaks and beetroot *smørbrød* **82**, 83
   the Pink Pick-me-up **44**, 45
   poached egg, mushroom and beetroot
   salad 160, **161**
Bergensk fiskesuppe 144, **145**
berries: fruit of the forest jam 19
   fruit of the forest and star anise

sorbet **184**, 185
   iced Nordic berries with white chocolate and
   cardamom sauce 196, **197**
   on-the-run morning muesli slice 26, **27**
   see also blackberries; blackcurrants;
   blueberries; raspberries; strawberries
bircher muesli for spring and summer 22
biscuits: *kokosmakroner* 133
   saffransskorpor 132
black and blue(berry) smoothie 28, **29**
blackberries: black and blue(berry)
   smoothie 28, **29**
   blackberry, almond and cardamom
   cake 116, **117**
blackcurrants: blackcurrant ice cream 186
   blackcurrant jam 18
Bloody Mary 42, *43*
blueberries: black and blue(berry)
   smoothie 28, **29**
   Mustikkapiirakka **126**, 127
   queen's compote 10, **11**
   spiced blueberry juice 111
   Bømlokake 121
borage: chilled cucumber and borage soup 147
bread 74
   cinnamon and chestnut bread 54–5, **54**
   fastelavensboller **136**, 137
   Mustikkapiirakka **126**, 127
   oatmeal bread 76–7, **76**
   spelt and fennel seed bread 78–9, **78**
broccoli: Mama Johansen's vegetable soup 96, **97**
brownies: Valhalla brownies 201
brunost: Daim cake 125
   grilled *brunost* on toast 61

cabbage: crunchy salad with lemon and
   mustard 100–1
   spiced lingonberry red cabbage 169
cakes: blackberry, almond and cardamom
   cake 116, **117**
   Daim cake 125
   drømmekage 120–1
   kladdkaka 124
   Mor Monsen 119
   spiced apple cake 115
   tropisk aroma **122**, 123

caramel: *Daim* caramel sauce 190
cardamom: banana and cardamom ice
   cream 187
   blackberry, almond and cardamom
    cake 116, **117**
   cream of tomato and cardamom soup 98
   fastelavensboller **136**, 137
   iced Nordic berries with white chocolate and
    cardamom sauce 196, **197**
celeriac: mussels with sherry, celeriac and
   tarragon **158**, 159
cheese: *Daim* cake 125
   egg, beetroot and cottage cheese salad 101
   goat's cheese with radish and rosehip
    smørbrød 80, **81**
   grilled *brunost* on toast 61
   grilled *Jarlsberg* on toast 173
   Jarlsberg and fennel muffins **62**, 63
   meatball gravy 169
   Nordic club sandwich **92**, 93
   roast asparagus with *Västerbotten* cheese 60
   Scandilicious macaroni cheese 166, **167**
   wild garlic and *Västerbotten* omelette 172
cheesecake: Norwegian cheesecake with tipsy
   strawberries **198**, 199
cherries: fruit of the forest jam 19
   sour cherry soup **194**, 195
   Valhalla brownies 201
chestnuts: cinnamon and chestnut
   bread 54–5, **54**
chicken: chicken liver pâté with pickled beetroot
   smørbrød 90
   Nordic club sandwich **92**, 93
   roast allspice chicken 165
chilled cucumber and borage soup 147
chocolate: banana, coconut and chocolate
   milkshake 47
   Bømlokake 121
   chocolate mocha coconut muffins 130, **131**
   Daim cake 125
   Daim caramel sauce 190
   hot chocolate shot 110
   iced Nordic berries with white chocolate and
    cardamom sauce 196, **197**
   kladdkaka 124
   saffransskorpor 132
   tropisk aroma **122**, 123
   Valhalla brownies 201
choux buns 134–5, **134**

cinnamon: arme riddere cinnamon toast with
   strawberries and cream 56, **57**
   banana and cinnamon crispbread 32, **33**
   cinnamon and chestnut bread 54–5, **54**
   cinnamon spelt pancakes 51
classic herring and potato *smørbrød* 88
clementines: the Pink Pick-me-up **44**, 45
club sandwich **92**, 93
coconut: banana, coconut and chocolate
   milkshake 47
   chocolate mocha coconut muffins 130, **131**
   cream of tomato and cardamom soup 98
   drømmekage 120–1
   kokosmakroner 133
   strawberry, orange and coconut smoothie 28
cod: salting 150
coffee: chocolate mocha coconut
   muffins 130, **131**
compotes: apples 13
   queen's compote 10, **11**
   rhubarb and orange compote 12
   spiced prune compote 14, **15**
cottage cheese: egg, beetroot and cottage cheese
   salad 101
crayfish soup 146
cream of tomato and cardamom soup 98
crunchy salad with lemon and mustard 100–1
crushed pea, bacon and tarragon *smørbrød* 91
cucumber: chilled cucumber and borage
   soup 147
the Green Goddess **44**, 45
currants: *Mor Monsen* 119

Daim and clotted cream ice cream sundae 191
Daim cake 125
Daim caramel sauce 190
dill: *gravlaks* with dill mustard sauce 151
   Scandinavian Bloody Mary 42, **43**
   tangy egg and potato salad 99
drinks: banana, coconut and chocolate
   milkshake 47
   black and blue(berry) smoothie 28, **29**
   the Green Goddess **44**, 45
   hot chocolate shot 110
   Pink Pick-me-up **44**, 45
   raspberry and rhubarb lemonade 46
   raspberry, vanilla and ginger smoothie 30
   Scandilicious gløgg 112
   Scandinavian Bloody Mary 42, **43**

spiced blueberry juice 111
strawberry, orange and coconut smoothie 28
drømmekage 120–1

eggs: baked eggs with anchovy and allspice 64
chopped egg and kaviar *smørbrød* 87
egg and anchovy soldiers **34**, 35
egg, beetroot and cottage cheese salad 101
eggs Norwegian 58–9
poached egg, mushroom and beetroot
salad 160, **161**
tangy egg and potato salad 99
wild garlic and *Västerbotten* omelette 172
ekte geitost: meatball gravy 169

fastelavensboller **136**, 137
fennel: crunchy salad with lemon and
mustard 100–1
mackerel, fennel and horseradish *smørbrød* 84
fennel seeds: *Jarlsberg* and fennel muffins **62**, 63
spelt and fennel seed bread 78–9, **78**
fish: baked eggs with anchovy and allspice 64
baked trout in crème fraiche 156, **156**
Bergensk fiskesuppe 144, **145**
chopped egg and kaviar *smørbrød* 87
classic herring and potato *smørbrød* 88
curing 150
egg and anchovy soldiers **34**, 35
eggs Norwegian 58–9
gravlaks and beetroot *smørbrød* **82**, 83
gravlaks with dill mustard sauce 151
grilled mackerel with kale, potatoes and
gooseberries 157
hot smoked trout salad 102, **103**
Janssons frestelse **162**, 163
mackerel, fennel and horseradish *smørbrød* 84
pickled herring 154, **155**
salt cod 150
smoked salmon tartare 65
speedy citrus-cured halibut 152
see also shellfish
French toast 56, **57**
fruit of the forest and star anise sorbet **184**, 185
fruit of the forest jam 19

garlic: wild garlic and *Västerbotten* omelette 172
ginger: beetroot and ginger soup 148, **149**
Green Goddess **44**, 45
raspberry, vanilla and ginger smoothie 30

gløgg 112
goat's cheese: goat's cheese with radish and
rosehip *smørbrød* 80, **81**
meatball gravy 169
gooseberries: grilled mackerel with kale,
potatoes and gooseberries 157
granola: sweet 'n' crispy rye granola 21
grapefruit: Pink Pick-me-up **44**, 45
gravlaks: *gravlaks* and beetroot *smørbrød* **82**, 83
gravlaks with dill mustard sauce 151
gravy: meatball gravy 169
Green Goddess **44**, 45
grilled *brunost* on toast 61
grilled *Jarlsberg* on toast 173
grilled mackerel with kale, potatoes and
gooseberries 157
grøt: Nordic porridge for autumn and winter 24
risengrynsgrøt 200
rømmegrøt 174

halibut: speedy citrus-cured halibut 152
hazelnuts: *Toscakake* 121
herrings: classic herring and potato *smørbrød* 88
pickled herring 154, **155**
hollandaise 59
honey: vanilla-infused honey **20**, 21
horseradish: mackerel, fennel and horseradish
smørbrød 84
hot chocolate shot 110
hot smoked trout salad 102, **103**

ice cream 182
banana and cardamom ice cream 187
blackcurrant ice cream 186
Daim and clotted cream ice cream sundae 191
lemon and nutmeg *krumkaker* 188–9, **188**
iced Nordic berries with white chocolate and
cardamom sauce 196, **197**

jams: blackcurrant jam 18
fruit of the forest jam 19
plum jam 16, **17**
Janssons frestelse **162**, 163
Jarlsberg: grilled *Jarlsberg* on toast 173
Jarlsberg and fennel muffins **62**, 63
Nordic club sandwich **92**, 93
Scandilicious macaroni cheese 166, **167**
jelly **202**, 203
lingonberry jelly with macerated

strawberries 204–5
juniper salt 152

kale: grilled mackerel with kale, potatoes and
    gooseberries 157
kaviar: chopped egg and kaviar *smørbrød* 87
kladdkaka 124
knickerbocker glory 48, **49**
kohlrabi: crunchy salad with lemon and
    mustard 100–1
kokosmakroner 133
krumkaker 188–9, **188**
kveldsmat evening pancakes 170, **171**

lamb: Norwegian meatballs 168
leeks: leek butter 150
    Mama Johansen's vegetable soup 96, **97**
lemons: crunchy salad with lemon and
    mustard 100–1
    lemon and nutmeg *krumkaker* 188–9, **188**
    lemony choux buns 134–5, **134**
    Mor Monsen 119
    raspberry and rhubarb lemonade 46
    speedy citrus-cured halibut 152
lingonberries: lingonberry jelly with macerated
    strawberries 204–5
    moose with chanterelles and lingonberry
    sauce 164
    spiced lingonberry red cabbage 169
liver: chicken liver pâté with pickled beetroot
    smørbrød 90

macaroni: Scandilicious macaroni
    cheese 166, **167**
macaroons: *kokosmakroner* 133
mackerel: grilled mackerel with kale, potatoes
    and gooseberries 157
    mackerel, fennel and horseradish *smørbrød* 84
Mama Johansen's plum muffins 128, **129**
Mama Johansen's vegetable soup 96, **97**
mansikkalumi 193
mashed swede and potato 169
meatballs: meatball baguette 94
    meatball gravy 169
    Norwegian meatballs 168
milkshakes: banana, coconut and chocolate
    milkshake 47
moose with chanterelles and lingonberry
    sauce 164

Mor Monsen 119
muesli: bircher muesli for spring and summer 22
    on-the-run morning muesli slice 26, **27**
muffins: chocolate mocha coconut muffins
    130, **131**
    Jarlsberg and fennel muffins **62**, 63
    Mama Johansen's plum muffins 128, **129**
    raspberry crunch muffins 50
mushrooms: moose with chanterelles and
    lingonberry sauce 164
    poached egg, mushroom and beetroot
    salad 160, **161**
    wild mushroom and tarragon *smørbrød* 85
mussels with sherry, celeriac and
    tarragon **158**, 159
mustard: crunchy salad with lemon and
    mustard 100–1
    gravlaks with dill mustard sauce 151
Mustikkapiirakka **126**, 127

Nordic club sandwich **92**, 93
Nordic porridge for autumn and winter 24
Norwegian cheesecake with tipsy
    strawberries **198**, 199
Norwegian knickerbocker glory 48, **49**
Norwegian meatballs 168
nutmeg: lemon and nutmeg *krumkaker*
    188–9, **188**

oats: bircher muesli for spring and summer 22
    Nordic porridge for autumn and winter 24
    oatmeal bread 76–7, **76**
omelettes: wild garlic and *Västerbotten*
    omelette 172
on-the-run morning muesli slice 26, **27**
onions: crispy 90
oranges: rhubarb and orange compote 12
    strawberry, orange and coconut smoothie 28

pancakes: cinnamon spelt pancakes 51
    kveldsmat evening pancakes 170, **171**
pasta: Scandilicious macaroni cheese 166, **167**
pâté: chicken liver pâté with pickled beetroot
    smørbrød 90
pearl barley porridge 25
peas: crushed pea, bacon and tarragon
    smørbrød 91
pickled herring 154, **155**
Pink Pick-me-up **44**, 45

plums: Mama Johansen's plum muffins 128, **129**
  plum jam 16, **17**
poached egg, mushroom and beetroot
  salad 160, **161**
pollack: *Bergensk fiskesuppe* 144, **145**
porridge: Nordic porridge for autumn and
  winter 24
  pearl barley porridge 25
  risengrynsgrøt 200
  rømmegrøt 174
potatoes: classic herring and potato *smørbrød* 88
  grilled mackerel with kale, potatoes and
    gooseberries 157
  Janssons frestelse **162**, 163
  Mama Johansen's vegetable soup 96, **97**
  mashed swede and potato 169
  tangy egg and potato salad 99
prawns: *Bergensk fiskesuppe* 144, **145**
  prawns on the rocks 66, **67**
  Toast Skagen 86
prunes: spiced prune compote 14, **15**

queen's compote 10, **11**

radishes: goat's cheese with radish and rosehip
  smørbrød 80, **81**
ramsons: wild garlic and *Västerbotten*
  omelette 172
raspberries: Pink Pick-me-up **44**, 45
  queen's compote 10, **11**
  raspberry and rhubarb lemonade 46
  raspberry crunch muffins 50
  raspberry, vanilla and ginger smoothie 30
red cabbage: spiced lingonberry red cabbage 169
rhubarb: rhubarb and orange compote 12
  raspberry and rhubarb lemonade 46
rice: *risengrynsgrøt* 200
risengrynsgrøt 200
roast allspice chicken 165
roast asparagus with *Västerbotten* cheese 60
rømmegrøt: Nordic porridge for autumn and
  winter 24
  Norwegian sour cream porridge 174
rosehip: goat's cheese with radish and rosehip
  smørbrød 80, **81**
rye: sweet 'n' crispy rye granola 21
  tilslørte bondepiker 192

saffransskorpor 132

saffron: *saffransskorpor* 132
salads: crunchy salad with lemon and
  mustard 100–1
  egg, beetroot and cottage cheese salad 101
  hot smoked trout salad 102, **103**
  poached egg, mushroom and beetroot
    salad 160, **161**
  tangy egg and potato salad 99
salmon: *Bergensk fiskesuppe* 144, **145**
  eggs Norwegian 58–9
  gravlaks and beetroot *smørbrød* **82**, 83
  gravlaks with dill mustard sauce 151
  smoked salmon tartare 65
salt cod 150
sandwiches: meatball baguette 94
  Nordic club sandwich **92**, 93
  see also *smørbrød*
sauces: *Daim* caramel sauce 190
  dill mustard sauce 151
  hollandaise 59
scallops: *Bergensk fiskesuppe* 144, **145**
Scandilicious *gløgg* 112
Scandilicious macaroni cheese 166, **167**
Scandinavian Bloody Mary 42, **43**
semlor **136**, 137
semolina: *rømmegrøt* 174
shellfish: *Bergensk fiskesuppe* 144, **145**
  crayfish soup 146
  mussels with sherry, celeriac and
    tarragon **158**, 159
  prawns on the rocks 66, **67**
  Toast Skagen 86
sherry: mussels with sherry, celeriac and
  tarragon **158**, 159
smoked salmon tartare 65
smoothies: black and blue(berry) smoothie 28, **29**
  raspberry, vanilla and ginger smoothie 30
  strawberry, orange and coconut smoothie 28
smørbrød 80
  chicken liver pâté with pickled beetroot 90
  chopped egg and kaviar 87
  classic herring and potato 88
  crushed pea, bacon and tarragon 91
  goat's cheese with radish and rosehip 80, **81**
  gravlaks and beetroot 82, 83
  mackerel, fennel and horseradish 84
  Toast Skagen 86
  wild mushroom and tarragon 85
smörgåsbord 38

sorbets: fruit of the forest and star anise
    sorbet **184**, 185
  strawberry sorbet 183
soups: beetroot and ginger soup 148, **149**
  Bergensk fiskesuppe 144, **145**
  chilled cucumber and borage soup 147
  crayfish soup 146
  cream of tomato and cardamom soup 98
  Mama Johansen's vegetable soup 96, **97**
  roasted swede soup 95
  sour cherry soup **194**, 195
sour cherry soup **194**, 195
sour cream: Nordic porridge for autumn and
    winter 24
  rømmegrøt 174
  vanilla and sour cream waffles **52**, 53
spelt: cinnamon spelt pancakes 51
  spelt and fennel seed bread 78–9, **78**
spiced apple cake 115
spiced blueberry juice 111
spiced lingonberry red cabbage 169
spiced prune compote 14, **15**
sprats: baked eggs with anchovy and allspice 64
  Janssons frestelse **162**, 163
stock: allspice chicken stock 165
strawberries: *arme riddere* cinnamon toast with
    strawberries and cream 56, **57**
  lingonberry jelly with macerated
    strawberries 204–5
  mansikkalumi 193
  Norwegian cheesecake with tipsy
    strawberries **198**, 199
  strawberry, orange and coconut smoothie 28
  strawberry sorbet 183
sursild 154, **155**
Svecia: Scandilicious macaroni cheese 166, **167**
swede: mashed swede and potato 169
  roasted swede soup 95
sweet 'n' crispy rye granola 21

tangy egg and potato salad 99
tarragon: crushed pea, bacon and tarragon
    smørbrød 91
  mussels with sherry, celeriac and
    tarragon **158**, 159
  wild mushroom and tarragon *smørbrød* 85
tarts: *Mustikkapiirakka* **126**, 127
tilslørte bondepiker 192
  Norwegian knickerbocker glory 48, **49**

Toast Skagen 86
tomatoes: cream of tomato and cardamom
    soup 98
  Scandinavian Bloody Mary 42, **43**
Toscakake 121
trifle: Norwegian knickerbocker glory 48, **49**
  tilslørte bondepiker 192
tropisk aroma **122**, 123
trout: baked trout in crème fraiche 156, **156**
  hot smoked trout salad 102, **103**

Valhalla brownies 201
vanilla: raspberry, vanilla and ginger smoothie
    30
  risengrynsgrøt 200
  vanilla and sour cream waffles **52**, 53
  vanilla salt 24
  vanilla-infused honey **20**, 21
Västerbotten: roast asparagus with *Västerbotten*
    cheese 60
  Scandilicious macaroni cheese 166, **167**
  wild garlic and *Västerbotten* omelette 172
veal: Norwegian meatballs 168

waffles: vanilla and sour cream waffles **52**, 53
wild garlic and *Västerbotten* omelette 172
wild mushroom and tarragon *smørbrød* 85
wine: *gløgg* 112

yoghurt 8–9

First published in Great Britain in 2011 by Saltyard Books
An imprint of Hodder & Stoughton
An Hachette UK company

1

A CIP catalogue record for this title is available from the British Library.

ISBN 978 1 444 70392 4

Typeset in Granjon and Mrs Eaves
Design by www.cabinlondon.co.uk
Colour reproduction by FMG
Food and props stylist Polly Webb-Wilson
Copy editor Bryony Nowell
Proof reader Margaret Gilbey
Indexer Caroline Wilding

Printed and bound in China by C&C Offset Printing Co Ltd

Hodder & Stoughton policy is to use papers that are natural, renewable and
recyclable products and made from wood grown in sustainable forests.
The logging and manufacturing processes are expected to conform to the
environmental regulations of the country of origin.

Hodder & Stoughton Ltd
338 Euston Road
London NW1 3BH

www.saltyardbooks.co.uk